Ecclesiastes

BIBLE STUDY COMMENTARY

Ecclesiastes

LOUIS GOLDBERG

 ZONDERVAN
PUBLISHING HOUSE
OF THE ZONDERVAN CORPORATION
GRAND RAPIDS, MICHIGAN 49506

ECCLESIASTES: BIBLE STUDY COMMENTARY

Copyright © 1983 by The Zondervan Corporation
Grand Rapids, Michigan

Library of Congress Cataloging in Publication Data

Goldberg, Louis, 1923-
    Ecclesiastes: Bible Study Commentary.

    Bibliography: p.
    1. Bible. O.T. Ecclesiastes—Commentaries.
I. Title
BS1475.3.G56   1983   223'.807   82-20069
ISBN 0-310-41823-2

Edited by Edward Viening

Printed in the United States of America

83 84 85 86 87 88 — 10 9 8 7 6 5 4 3 2

Contents

Preface

Many years ago when I was a young believer, a cultist attempted to prove to me that the Bible does not teach immortality. When I asked him for the source of his teaching, he quoted a number of passages from Ecclesiastes, principally 3:20, which declares that both animals and humans return to the dust after death. Instinctively, I felt that he was not pursuing a sound Bible exposition because other portions of the Scriptures do teach that the soul and spirit of humans are indestructible and continue to exist after the physical death of the person.

But when I tried to grasp what the writer of Ecclesiastes meant by the statements in 3:19 and 20, I felt somewhat at a loss to reconcile how people came from the dust and returned there again with the assertion that while we die and our bodies return to the dust, yet our spirit returns to God (12:7), perhaps suggesting that we no longer existed and so God reclaimed the spirit once again.

In addition, I have reflected across the years on what I had been taught concerning the writer of Ecclesiastes who was "only talking about the wisdom of this world" and was *only* seeing things from "under the sun." (Until we have identified the person responsible for the authorship of the book, we shall refer to him as the "writer.") It seemed to me that with this view there is the taint of "sub-inspiration" attached to the book because it deals *only* with matters of this world that are not important, although every Bible teacher will insist that, after all, Ecclesiastes is part of the canon. What further compounded the problem of understanding this book for me was when Bible teachers explained that even as the Word of God accurately records the lie that Satan told Eve (Gen. 3:4), so somehow the writer of Eccle-

7

siastes was only handling half-truths or untruths of the accepted spiritual life as God wants it.

All of these conflicting observations set me on a search for answers to what the writer of Ecclesiastes was trying to say. I read the book again and again, comparing it with the other wisdom books of the Bible and trying to find a more satisfying way to understand it. I wanted to know the writer's purpose and intent in portraying the life on earth that can be enjoyed as God designed it but also examining the frailties of life that both unbeliever and believer will experience in this world.

Through the years I have served as a pastor and teacher and have traveled much, and during all that time I have found that people everywhere have numerous questions about the problems of life and the existence of God. While many have their pros and cons about whether or not there is a personal God, most people stop short of actually denying His existence and even His presence. There is a kind of furtive backward glance over the shoulder that perhaps senses or hears His footsteps although it is a mystery to many as to where He might be found.

Most people, as they reflect on life from their experiences, say that life at its best is really only one big mystery. Life is supposed to be a bowl of cherries, but many claim they are in the "pits"! Why does God, if He exists, permit catastrophes to happen, such as the killing of people in war or through natural disasters? Why do as many as 100,000 people die suddenly in an earthquake? Why do people fall ill? Why are children inflicted with incurable diseases and die before they even have an opportunity to live something of what this life has to offer? Is there really any meaning to life? Even though in one sense it may be a big question, most people try to extract some joy and pleasure from this life with their families, in traveling, and in pursuing what passes for delight in this world.

It seems to me that Ecclesiastes speaks to us where we are. Being on the same level with the rest of mankind, the writer seeks to explore the many facets of life and asks the questions many others are thinking. What does it mean to work, seemingly find no joy in it, and end up in meaninglessness, especially if we work all of our lifetime and, because of unforeseen circumstances, are not able to pass the fruit of our labors on to our children? Does it really pay to live godly and piously in this world if we see the wicked enjoying themselves while the righteous suffer all the more? Where is real wisdom to be found? Can an ultimate wisdom be found? Out of his many experiences, the writer of Ecclesiastes says positively that while he cannot get at the essence of wisdom, he perceives a wisdom from God that will help us in the midst of the many particulars of this life.

In many ways, the writer of Ecclesiastes struggled with the same kinds of questions Job did. Even as Job looked for meaning to life in the midst of his desperate illness, so the writer of Ecclesiastes also sighed and groaned, cried out and hung limp, but never despaired because of his trust and faith in God.

After years of wrestling with Ecclesiastes, I have come to feel that God does give to believers, as well as unbelievers, many of the answers to how to live in this world. While I do not intend to deal with all questions of the life of believers in their relationship with God (because this is not the purpose of the book), yet we can find the best possible advice in how to understand many of life's realities and cope with them. This book is written with the hope that believers will, in their maturing relationships with the living God, find that advice from Ecclesiastes to enable them to see life a little more clearly and, in the process, relate to others who are struggling to find answers to life.

Acknowledgments

I want to acknowledge with the deepest of appreciation eager students from whom I have learned as we discussed Ecclesiastes. I am grateful for the numerous opportunities to share this book with many people who were searching for the meaning to life and who wanted to know if it was possible to know a living God in the midst of the pressures, sorrows, mysteries, and joys of this world. I express my sincerest appreciation to Corinna Leal and Beverly James who typed the first draft and to Mrs. Lin Johnson who edited and typed the final copy. Even as we are reminded by the Teacher in Ecclesiastes to have the keenest delight in one's wife (9:9) and that she is a gift of God to a man in the midst of the trials and problems of this life, so I deeply appreciate my wife's encouragement while I was involved in the many hours of research and preparation of this manuscript.

Introduction

General

The three major books of wisdom in the Old Testament are Job, Proverbs, and Ecclesiastes. Written and collected by men who were the sages of Israel, Proverbs and Ecclesiastes particularly represent many facets of the wisdom of God and its accompanying experiences.

Most believers today are familiar with two particular offices in the Old Testament, that of the priest and the prophet. The former offered the sacrifices and in worship and prayer represented the people before God. The prophet, on the other hand, brought specific messages to the people of Israel and in a sense represented God to the people. But a third class of servants, not generally known, were the sages who gave advice based on the Word of God. These three offices are described by Jeremiah: "Come, let's make plans against Jeremiah; for the teaching of the law by the *priest* will not be lost, nor will counsel from the *wise*, nor the word from the *prophets*" (Jer. 18:18). The sages [wise ones] were an acknowledged group in Israel who performed a very important function in giving advice to which people had to give heed.

The wisdom that the sages presented is not the kind of wisdom with which philosophers were involved. Plato and others sought for the essence or ultimate in wisdom and attempted to get at it through human rationalizations, an effort that was carried on solely on the human level. The wisdom of the Old Testament, however, was provided by God through revelation to be accepted by the mind (rationale) and heart. It was not a wisdom designed to cater to a person's pride but to enable him to live a moral life. Wise advice, therefore, was given to people to help them make the right ethical choices that God asks them to do. In no way should this special kind of wisdom be dubbed as inferior because it has proven itself in the arena of life from the day it *was* given to meet adequately the problems of this world.

There is no doubt that we see at times the attempt by the sages to get at the mysterious and seemingly unattainable ultimate or essence of wisdom, even as many philosophers have sought to do. Ecclesiastes on a number of occasions reveals this attempt, but the effort is seen also in Proverbs where Solomon realized that an ultimate in wisdom does exist: "By wisdom the LORD laid the earth's foundations, by understanding he set the heavens in place" (Prov. 3:19). But the wisdom writers also understood that there was a veil between man living in this world and God as the ultimate wisdom in the heavens above; therefore, it was not possible to get at the essence of wisdom because God has not chosen to reveal everything within His divine plan. The Old Testament sages had enough experience with their knowledge of God that they were aware of a danger in trying to press the use of human rationalization too far. With what presuppositions and with which human reasoning can a person arrive to declare that he has total wisdom?

An intertestamental wisdom writer in the book of Ecclesiasticus expressed his apprehension with the attainment of total knowledge: "What is too wonderful for you, do not seek, nor search after what is hidden from you. Seek to understand what is permitted you, and have no concern with mysteries" (3:20f.). Although the Old Testament person had access only to the particulars of wisdom, he had some grasp on faith and morality that he definitely could attain. The person who grasps this kind of wisdom is wise indeed!

Having made these preliminary comments regarding wisdom, it must also be recognized that, because of the distinctive purpose and scope of Ecclesiastes, this book sets forth wisdom differently than what is proclaimed in Job, Proverbs, and some of the wisdom Psalms. There are many points of contact between all the wisdom literature to which we will allude when dealing with the text itself, but we recognize that the writer of Ecclesiastes had an explicit way of applying wisdom to the needs and problems of his everyday life. Its difference was noted by Renan, a French philosopher, who thought that it was the only charming book ever written by a Jew. Heinrich Heine, a Jewish poet of the Enlightenment, thought it was "the canticle of skepticism" because he felt that it bordered on skepticism, or the inability to find real wisdom. Franz Delitzsch in the introduction to his commentary on the book declared Ecclesiastes to be "the canticles of the fear of God." After reading the book, many people declare that there is a uniqueness to Ecclesiastes that has few parallels in ancient or modern religious literature.

Purpose and Theme

Every piece of literature should have a theme or purpose, and Ecclesiastes has its purpose and plan as well as a specific theme. However, it seems that as one peruses the book, the question arises, "Where is the purpose and theme to be found?" Since the book opens with the exclamation "Meaningless!" we might assume that there is a pessimism at the worst, or a doubt at the best, on the part of the writer who finds difficulty in dealing with his world. Such is not the case, however; and we have to search diligently to get at the basic message of the book in order to ascertain its purpose and theme.

We think it best to go immediately to the epilogue to learn a most important dimension to what the writer is trying to say. While there are those who insist that the epilogue was added later by a scribe, or morals teacher, in order to touch up a seeming skepticism, we insist that the epilogue is very much in keeping with the message of the rest of the book.

One of the first basic areas of consideration is the statement to "fear God" (*elohim;* 12:13). This command is a parallel found in all of the wisdom literature: "The fear of the Lord—that is wisdom" (Job 28:28); "The fear of the LORD is the beginning of knowledge (Prov. 1:7); "The fear of the LORD is the beginning of wisdom" (Prov. 9:10); "The fear of the LORD teaches a man wisdom" (Prov. 15:33). This subject is also very much a part of Ecclesiastes (3:14; 5:7; 7:18; and 8:12–13, where it is mentioned six times). Therefore, we conclude that a major emphasis in Ecclesiastes is that we must have a reverential awe of God.

This emphasis to "fear God" is not peculiar to the wisdom literature. Moses had this theme as his basis for one's approach to God (i.e., Lev. 19:14, 32; 25:17, 36, 43; Deut. 4:10; 5:29; 6:2, 13, 24; 8:6). Numerous examples are found in the lives of other Old Testament people, such as Abraham (Gen. 22:12), the Hebrew midwives (Exod. 1:17, 21), and Job (28:28). These are only a few of the many who knew the key to the approach to God: fear (reverence, be in awe of) Him.

Another reason for having reverence toward God is to show respect for the careful analysis at an appointed time of our deeds by God, whether they are good or evil (12:14). This verse is not an isolated statement added by some pious writer but is one of the themes of Ecclesiastes. We are advised that God will bring us into judgment as to how we live our lives (11:9); at an appointed time God judges the righteous and the wicked (3:17); and the deeds of the righteous and of the wise are in the hands of God (9:1).

From the emphases of reverence toward God and having to give an account of ourselves some day before Him in another world, we have one of the major purposes of Ecclesiastes. Does this sound like a person who does not believe in immortality?

One reason for this care regarding how we live and the deeds that we do is that we have to realize we do fall short in our attainments: "This only have I found: God made mankind upright, but men have gone in search of many schemes" (7:29). The Hebrew word for "schemes," *hishevonot*, has the idea of thoughts, reckonings, and inventions. God made us upright in the sense that in our state of innocence we were morally straight; but after the Fall, we deviated from the moral righteousness of God, went our own way, and did our own "thing," all of which were against God's original intention. We have our schemes by which we stray from what we were originally.

How different is the conclusion of Platonic philosophy that teaches that if we know to do the right thing, we will do the right. The Bible in general and the writer of Ecclesiastes in particular knew better; we can make a mess of things even if we *know* the right thing to do. Given our bent to scheme to do wrong, we must never forget that we have to give an account to God some day. Therefore, we see another main purpose of the book in that we in this life need to keep God in the center of everything we do. While we may not be able to understand all that goes on in this world or what happens to us, we will be spared more grief in all our decisions and deeds if we always take to heart our accountability to and reverential awe of God.

Still another purpose of the book is to define our interests and pursuits and the way in which we are involved in them. The writer gave himself in particular to at least three areas in which he thought he could succeed in finding fulfillment: the intense study to gain wisdom (1:13–18), the hot pursuit of "wine, women, and song" and the pleasures that go with them (2:1–3), as well as the heavy involvement with the amassing of material things (2:4–11). His final assessment after he had given himself solely to each of these areas in succession was that any one interest to the exclusion of everything else is "meaningless." At first this might sound like the voice of a cynic or a pessimist. In no way is this true! If a person becomes merely a professional knowledge seeker or loses himself in immorality and laughter or lives only for what can be accumulated in this world, then he has perverted the very reason God created him. If any of these three areas, or any other area for that matter, is all we live for, then certainly life is empty. There has to be a better reason why God created us than just to gratify one interest only to the exclusion of all other pursuits.

Close on the heels of living entirely and solely for one interest is the possibility that God has given us many things to enjoy: 1) "A man can do nothing better than to eat and drink and find satisfaction in his work. This too, I see, is from the hand of God" (2:24); 2) "Enjoy life with your wife, whom you love" (9:9); and 3) "Go, eat your food with gladness, and drink your wine with a joyful heart, for it is now that God favors what you do" (9:7). This emphasis is repeated in a number of other portions of Ecclesiastes and suggests that this world has in it many dimensions that God has given us to enjoy. To ignore this feature or to declare that this world is no good is to completely misunderstand and even pervert God's intentions for what He designed for us. The encouragement to enjoy life clearly indicates that the writer was not a pessimist or a gloom-and-doom pusher. Therefore, we are not to make ourselves sick with any one interest to the exclusion of everything else because a one-track pursuit is meaningless. The antidote is to enjoy a wide variety of things in this world which are God's gifts to us. We can well say that one of the great purposes of Ecclesiastes is to recognize the need for balance in a person's life, a lesson that has to be learned by both believer and unbeliever.

The five purposes—1) fear God; 2) God will judge all our deeds after this life; 3) God must be kept in the center of life because it is so easy to go astray; 4) do not overdo any one interest to the exclusion of everything or everyone else; 5) enjoy life as a gift from God—all confirm that Ecclesiastes has its source in divine revelation. The observations of how to live in this world and do it in the best way possible can come only from a wisdom that God gives. God gave the writer a definite wisdom, and the lessons he learned through his experiences are priceless gems given for our fulfillment as created beings.

With these purposes in mind, what can we understand to be the theme of the book? In examining what different commentators have to say about the theme, we find a variety of suggestions. Possibly this diversity results from an undue emphasis on any one area; and therefore many of the themes suggested reflect a lopsided view of the book. With moderation as one of the purposes, we cannot accept the extreme views of themes for Ecclesiastes as either pessimistic where the writer is a doomsday person or as hedonistic where worldly pleasures are the best pursuit for mankind.

It seems to this author that the theme can come only from a statement that the writer made, "He [God] has made everything beautiful in its time. He has also set eternity in the hearts of men; yet they cannot fathom what God has done from beginning to end" (3:11). This verse is discussed later when dealing with the text, but note the two key points: first, we have a grasp of eternity (ʿolam). Although we live in this world and are caught up with its pressures and strains, pushes and pulls, and joys and sorrows, we do have an instinctive feel that there is something beyond this life. The writer sensed that God has a plan that includes everything that happens from the vantage point of eternity where we will find ourselves one day. The only way to try to discover what goes on in this world is to realize that God does have an overall plan.

Second, we are caught up in the things of this world and are looking for answers to the reasons for events; often we feel hopeless and helpless in getting at the meaning of life. The point is that no one thing, area, or person in this world is able to provide ultimate answers, or at times even partial answers, as to why everything takes the course it does. How can we, for example, deal with the prosperity of the wicked and the suffering of the righteous (7:14–15)? How can we understand why we can work an entire lifetime and yet lose whatever we have accumulated, sometimes almost in an instant (6:1–4)? Other strange circumstances happen that can tear at the heart of a person. So it appears that the basic theme for the book is to realize that God has a total plan for all events that occur, that we can understand that such a plan does exist, and we have to look to God for answers. Yet we also know that we can find only partial answers in this world.

This theme was illustrated when a wealthy man gave us a firsthand look at a beautiful Persian rug in his salon. The pattern was exquisite, and no one less than a genius could have contrived such a beautiful design, but then this man lifted up the carpet and let us see what was on the underside. It was possible to make out something of the design on the topside, but there was also a hopeless tangle of thread and color that prevented us from appreciating the entire design. The man was a believer who had tasted much of this world's sorrows, and he used this rug to explain his experiences with life. As God sees what takes place in this world, He knows what is going on in accordance to His plan, just as we saw the beautiful design of the rug. However, as we see it from our perspective, like the underside of the rug, we can only sense that there is a plan but we are not able to see and make out all of the details. With this theme and purpose in mind, we can have a positive outlook on life, a moral to follow, and a sense of immortality after leaving this world.

Consequently, we can understand another of the writer's statements in his epilogue conclusion. In no way is life meaningless; rather, we are to "Fear God and keep his commandments, for this is the whole duty of man" (12:13). The last line reads literally, "for this is all of man," suggesting that when it is all said and done, God is interested in the whole personality of a man and woman whereby each one finds complete fulfillment in life. As long as we understand the theme and internalize the purposes of Ecclesiastes, we will have the fullness God intended for our personalities.

The Title of the Book and Name of the Principal Character: Qohelet

The English title Ecclesiastes is derived from the Septuagint, the Greek translation of the Old Testament. The Hebrew word behind the Greek is *qohelet*, which appears seven times in the book and is the term by which the writer describes himself (1:1, 2, 12; 7:27; 12:8, 9, 10). The word itself is an active feminine participle that comes from the Hebrew verb *qahal*, meaning "to call." *Qohelet* in one sense can refer to the office, that is, the preacher's office. In another sense, the word has been applied to the individual who holds the office. Technically, we can say that *qohelet* is a reference to the one who calls the people together in an assembly, but in usage the word has come to be applied to the one who also teaches or preaches in the assembly. That is why the Septuagint uses *ecclesiastes*, meaning "preacher." In many translations the word appears as "preacher," while the NIV uses "Teacher."

The point, then, is that this individual fulfills the office of the sage or wise man; and his object is to teach wisdom as given to him by God and as he learns it in his own experience. He also wishes to impart this wisdom to others who might learn from his mistakes so as to live wisely, in a spiritual sense, a God-honoring life in this world.

It is interesting to note that in the course of Jewish tradition, it became the practice that continues to this day that Ecclesiastes is read every year on the third day of the Feast of Tabernacles (*sukkot*), which comes at the end of September or in October. In ancient Israel, Tabernacles had as one emphasis celebration with great joy that the general harvest had been gathered in. Perhaps this practice began when Ezra read the Law in front of the water gate and a revival broke out with people weeping due to conviction of sin (Neh. 8–9). With hearts made tender by the reading of the Word, the Levites then told the people, "Do not mourn or weep. . . . Go and enjoy choice food and sweet drinks, and send some to those who have nothing prepared. The day is sacred to our Lord. Do not grieve, for the joy of the LORD is your strength" (Neh. 8:9–10). Therefore, when the people had built their booths on this occasion, there was an air of joy and happiness, a practice continued in succeeding generations. The tradition brings out the truth that the writer of Ecclesiastes wanted to convey: Life is a gift from God for us to enjoy provided we keep everything in moderation. Interestingly, the word for joy (*simḥah*) and the verb from which it comes (*samaḥ*), meaning "to be glad, to rejoice," occur seventeen times in the book.

Author and Date

The name of the author behind *Qohelet* never once appears in this book. But the writer included clues to his identity: "The words of the Teacher, son of David, king in Jerusalem" (1:1) and "I, the Teacher, was king over Israel in Jerusalem" (1:12). From this data it was assumed that Solomon was intended since he was the direct successor to the throne of David. The evidence for this king is substantiated by the references to the person who had great wisdom (1:16), tremendous wealth (2:8), involvement in great building accomplishments (2:4–6), and a huge retinue of servants (2:7), all of which adequately describe Solomon. Jewish scholarship, therefore, held that Solomon was the author of Ecclesiastes, and the traditions indicate that "Hezekiah and his company wrote Ecclesiastes" (Baba Bathra 15a, Talmud, which could mean that Hezekiah in the days of his literary accomplishment merely edited and published the text). Other Jewish traditions declare directly that Solomon was the author; see Megilla 7a; Shabbath 30 in the Talmud.

Before Ecclesiastes was accepted into the canon, there was a running argument between two groups of scholars in Israel in the first century B.C. Those of Shammai questioned canonicity, while those of Hillel accepted the book; eventually the latter prevailed and the book was recognized as canonical, that is, "it defiles the hands ritually," a phrase indicating that the Scriptures came from God and therefore must be treated with the greatest of respect. In the Hebrew Bible, Ecclesiastes is part of what is called the Megillot (rolls) in the third division, the Writings. (The Megillot consists of Song of Songs, Ruth, Lamentations, Ecclesiastes, and Esther in that order.)

For centuries the early church and that of the Middle Ages accepted Solomonic authorship and canonicity. The critical view that denies the authorship of Solomon did not become the vogue until the nineteenth century, although Luther felt that Solomon did not actually write the book; rather, others among the sages and learned men took the words from Solomon and framed them in the form of the text as we have it today. Most Protestant scholars at the end of the nineteenth and on into the twentieth century do not hold to a Solomonic authorship: "If the book of Kohelet were of old Solomonic origin, then there is no history of the Hebrew language," F. Delitzsch, "Ecclesiastes," *Commentaries on the Song of Songs and Ecclesiastes* (Grand Rapids: Eerdmans [1950], p. 190). "In all probability the book is to be dated about the time of Malachi," E. J. Young, *Introduction to the Old Testament* (Grand Rapids: Eerdmans [1949], p. 369). Modern Jewish scholarship concurs: "The view that Solomon is the author has been universally abandoned today, with the growth of a truer recognition of the style, vocabulary and world-outlook of Qohelet," R. Gordis, *Qohelet, The Man and His World* (New York: Schocken [1971], p. 5).

The authorship is denied for a number of reasons. The name Solomon does not appear at all in the text of the book, and all the other works of Solomon do bear his name (Proverbs, Song of Songs, and some of his Psalms, i.e., 72 and 127). If Solomon claimed authorship for the other books, why did he not do so for Ecclesiastes? Therefore, Qohelet appears as the ideal Teacher of wisdom.

Another argument against Solomonic authorship is the way the text reads, "I, the Teacher, *was* king over Israel in Jerusalem" (1:12). The claim is that the verb "was" is the perfect tense of the verb "to be" *(hayiti)*; therefore, Solomon was no longer king when Ecclesiastes was put together. But this is an unfair assessment. In later Hebrew the verb form can be applied to past events, but in many biblical texts the idea can be, "I was and still am," as illustrated by Moses' statement when Gershom was born, "I have become *(hayiti)* an alien in a foreign land" (Exod. 2:22) and the assertion by Jacob's sons as they stood before Joseph whom they did not recognize, "Your servants are *(hayiti)* honest men, not spies" (Gen. 42:11). The use of the verb can be put into a present understanding; and therefore, Solomon could have said either "I have been king" or "I am king." This understanding appears to settle the case on the basis of the text.

A third argument suggests that it is impossible for Solomon to be the author because there is a question as to whom he would be comparing his wisdom, "I have grown and increased in wisdom more than anyone who has ruled over Jerusalem before me" (1:16). Since David was his immediate predecessor with acumen for wisdom, then with whom is a supposed Solomon comparing himself? But Solomon could be comparing himself to David and a long line of Canaanite kings who ruled in the land for centuries before Solomon, such as Melchizedek (Gen. 14:18) and Adoni-Zedek (Josh. 10:1), a view suggested by E. Hengstenberg in *Commentary on Ecclesiastes* (tr. by D. W. Sim, Philadelphia: Smith, English [1869], pp. 60–61). In fact, the text of 1:16 itself does not refer to any king prior to Solomon, but rather to "all," to "anyone." His comparison was with the wise people who had anything to say in the leadership of the city. The people in 1 Kings 4:31, Ethan, Heman, Calcol, and Darda, no doubt wise men in Jerusalem before Solomon, and Melchizedek could be included in this group. (See G. Archer, *A Survey of Old Testament Introduction*, Chicago: Moody Press [1964], p. 469.) Therefore, the supposed problem of trying to fit 1:16 into the days of Solomon is not as serious as it appears.

By far the most serious argument against the Solomonic authorship is the kind of Hebrew used in the text that would supposedly place the book in the postexilic period, fifth century B.C. Even such conservative scholars as F. Delitzsch, E. J. Young, and H. Leupold hold to this point of view. Some of the more critical scholars want to date Ecclesiastes even later in the Greek period during the time of the Maccabees, second century B.C. They claim that the language of Ecclesiastes is completely unlike any other literature of the tenth century B.C. because of so-called Aramaisms as well as Hebrew grammatical structure that can only place the book in the postexilic period or later.

An older critical view at the end of the 1800s asserted that the presence of Aramaisms, Aramaic words and grammatical structure, was always a sure sign of the later Persian period (about 300s B.C.), the Greek period (about 200–100 B.C.), and even in some instances the Roman period (first centuries B.C. and A.D.). The archaeological evidence of our century, however, demonstrates that Aramaisms abound in all the literature of the second and first *millenniums* B.C. Therefore, the older critical view is no longer valid. Mitchell Dahood suggests that Aramaisms are not necessarily an argument for late dating ("Canaanite-Phoenician influence in Qohelet," *Biblica*, 33 [1952], pp. 191–221) and even proposes concerning the book that some author of about 1,000 B.C. wrote in Hebrew but was influenced by the Canaanite-Phoenician language's many facets of grammar and vocabulary (G. Archer, p. 465). While this suggestion does not decisively prove that Solomon was the author, yet there were economic and political ties with Phoenicia during the Solomonic reign; the language influences on Hebrew were also strong. The traffic was also great with the Aramaic-speaking Syrians in Solomon's reign, which could explain the presence of Aramaisms in the *Qohelet* text.

In dealing further with the language structure of Ecclesiastes, Gleason Archer suggests that "the Hebrew of Ecclesiastes is quite as dissimilar to that of Malachi, Nehemiah and Esther as to any of the pre-exilic books" (p. 465). Both conservative and liberal scholars try to show that Ecclesiastes fits best with and is most similar to the postexilic biblical literature but as a rule do not show the dissimilarities. In addition, Archer argues against putting the book in the period of the Maccabees (second century B.C.) after the postexilic books because of the evidence of Qumran (Dead Sea Scrolls literature). He declares, "There are absolutely no affinities between the vocabulary or style of Ecclesiastes and that of the sectarian literature of Qumran community" (p. 465). The point is that Ecclesiastes has a specific language, grammar, and vocabulary that cannot be identified with any period of Hebrew history; it is unlike the literature of the tenth century B.C.; it is not like that of the writers of the early postexilic period; it does not fit into the Maccabean period; nor does it reflect an even later period in Jewish history of the first century or later. (See David S. Margoliouth, "The Book of Ecclesiastes," in *The Jewish Encyclopedia*, V, ed. Isador Singer, New York: Funk and Wagnalls [1901–1906], p. 33). Why can we not accept, as Archer suggested, that a particular literature developed in Israel that was unique and which allowed for an expression of wisdom peculiar to the author of a particular period (p. 466)? Even more compelling, however, are the many similarities found in the internal evidence between Ecclesiastes and the Book of Proverbs concerning the wisdom and fear of God, as well as the data of 1 Kings 1–11. We conclude that Solomon is the only one who can fit the situation; and since we know him to be a writer, he could have developed his own peculiar style, even as writers' styles vary across long periods of time. We accept Solomon writing under the title of Teacher as the author who had something to say regarding how we should live in this world.

Date of Writing During Solomon's Lifetime

At what most plausible time could Solomon have written Ecclesiastes? What would be the underlying reason for writing the book and sharing his wisdom?

We know that there were certain landmark experiences in Solomon's life: 1) when he was young and humble before the Lord he asked God for wisdom to rule Israel (1 Kings 3); 2) he had been referred to by another name, Jedidiah (2 Sam. 12:24–25), meaning "loved by the Lord," an apt description of God's choice individual whom He had placed on the throne of Israel; 3) when he had attained the zenith of his rule, he also tragically turned away from the Lord in attempting to please his pagan wives who were idolaters (1 Kings 11:9); 4) he had been warned to desist from his apostasy by the Lord (1 Kings 11:9–10); and finally, 5) God, in order to humiliate Solomon, raised up adversaries against him from a number of sources (1 Kings 11:14–26).

The question now arises as to whether or not the discipline of God had any effect on Solomon. There seems to be a hint to that possibility in that the wisdom of Solomon was with him to the end of his life (1 Kings 11:41–43). In addition, we are told that there is a book called "The Annals of Solomon" (v. 41); some have suggested that the text of Ecclesiastes is actually the substance of "The Annals." There is no way we can verify this statement, however, because this book does not exist at the present time.

Did Solomon repent because of the pressure God put on him? Why not? As we read the text of Ecclesiastes, we see that the Teacher could hardly have written it while still in apostasy. There is an "air of repentance" in the spirit of the writer. On the other hand, the book could not have been written prior to the apostasy period; rather, there appears in Ecclesiastes the evidence of a deep maturity of one who gives wise advice on how to live the best possible kind of life and how to avoid the extremes of life. We assume that one aspect of the extremes would have to be the undue interest in pagan women, which was one reason for Solomon's downfall. There is also the description in great detail of the advancing years and the infirmities of old age (12:2–6). Of course, any person who is a good writer can put together a vivid story of how a person ages; it would seem, however, that the Teacher was speaking out of personal experience. Therefore, it appears that the breath of repentance, the depth of wisdom expressed for many facets of life, and the spirit of humility before God mark the time of writing as being after the author's period of apostasy.

Did not God deal with other kings so as to bring them back to Himself? Is not Manasseh a good example of how God had to drastically discipline an extremely rebellious son of his godly father Hezekiah? It took the prison of a foreign land to bring Manasseh to his senses (2 Chron. 33:10–13). How God can discipline us likewise! It appears that He had taken drastic action with Solomon; and at the end of his life, David's son was able to speak from his wisdom as well as from the depths of an experience of suffering and humiliation.

One puzzling feature in Ecclesiastes, and decidedly a serious question concerning one who had been restored by the Lord, is the complete lack of the use of God's covenant name with Israel, Yahweh. Instead, Solomon used the general name of God, Elohim, which expresses His power and creatorship. In addition, Solomon did not talk about God's mercies to Israel under the name of "Yahweh who cares for His people." Concerning this reference to God's loving relationship to His people, we can simply reply that Solomon had other purposes for the book; and we must not insist that we have to read every theological idea of the Old Testament into the Book of Ecclesiastes, thereby insisting that the Teacher has to wax eloquent on God's mercy. Likewise, we do not declare the writer of Ecclesiastes an atheist because the covenant name of God does not appear at all in the text.

More serious, however, is the sole use of Elohim, twenty-eight times in the book, which might mark some spiritual lack in the Teacher. But when people raise questions concerning why Solomon did or did not use certain names of God, perhaps they miss God's intentions concerning Israel from the beginning to be a testimony to

God in the midst of a sea of pagan nations. Already at the end of his life, Moses had instructed, "See, I have taught you decrees and laws as the LORD my God commanded me, so that you may follow them in the land you are entering to take possession of it. Observe them carefully, for this will show your wisdom and understanding *to the nations*, who will hear about all these decrees and say, 'Surely this great nation is a wise and understanding people'" (Deut. 4:5–6). While it was not the primary intention that individuals of the people of Israel go to other pagan nations and be "missionaries," nevertheless, the blessing of God on His people would be in such proportion that it would attract the pagan nations to consider who this God of Israel was.

The point is that the pagan nations, when talking about the God of Israel, used a name that was most prevalent across the Middle East, "El," from which Elohim was a derivative and in the plural. Pagans would certainly not talk in terms of "Yahweh," which was the covenant name of God with His people Israel. Therefore, one of the reasons why Solomon used Elohim exclusively was to perhaps relate to people where they were and talk about a wisdom that not only applied to the people of Israel but also had an appeal to unsaved peoples. It is in this sense that even the Queen of Sheba came to the court of Solomon to learn from his wisdom, of which she had heard in her native land (1 Kings 10:1). We know that there was traffic from pagan nations to Jerusalem, and people came from far and wide to see for themselves what Israel had. Even as late as the New Testament, an Ethiopian official made the long, arduous, journey in order to worship before the Lord in Jerusalem (Acts 8:27). There is no way to begin to estimate the tremendous attraction that the worship in Jerusalem and the wisdom of the Old Testament, particularly that of Solomon, would have on those who were dissatisfied with their own religions and were also looking for basic answers to life.

The Unity of the Book

As we have already seen, for centuries neither Jewish nor Christian religious authorities questioned that Solomon was the author under the name of Qohelet. In the same way, no questions had been raised by these authorities as to the unity of the book. It is only in the modern period of the latter 1800s and this century that scholars claim this book is the product of various authors; for example, the seemingly negative statements are said to be from the hand of the original writer, while the more positive statements were added at a later date.

One answer to their assertions is that similar themes are mentioned throughout Ecclesiastes. For example, we note how prevalent are the subjects of the exhortation to fear God (already discussed), the fact that God will judge every man for his deeds during his lifetime (3:15; 5:6; 7:29; 8:5; etc.; see commentary for how these texts are handled), and the charge that man should gratefully receive the blessings of God as a gift from Him (2:24-26; 5:18-19; 8:15; 9:7-9).

However, simply tracing similar thought patterns through the entire book is not, from a modern critical point of view, the approach to demonstrate the unity of a book. Critics still insist that the original writer had a negative outlook on life, and therefore the book has been reworked so that both a negative and positive view on life are presented.

O. S. Rankin in his "Introduction and Exegesis" to Ecclesiastes (*The Interpreter's Bible*, V, Nashville: Abingdon Press [1956], pp. 7-8) gave an overview of some of the critical approaches of how this book supposedly has been put together by various people. One view has it that Ecclesiastes was originally a major work but that minor additions were provided. Wildeboer indicated in 1898 that the book was a unity, including the epilogue, to which some minor additions had been made. A later commentator, Hertzberg, while not accepting the epilogue as part of the original work, nevertheless agreed with Wildeboer to a large extent.

Another view is that there was a smaller, basic Ecclesiastes to which major additions have been added. Carl Siegfried suggested that there has been a negative Greek influence on the original author of Ecclesiastes. Sometime later, however, he proposed that a Hellenized, religious Jewish leader added some Epicurean content regarding the many encouragements to enjoy life. A still further addition was seen by Siegfried where one of Israel's sages, a *hakam*, provided the proverbs to support the wisdom given to Israel. Then along came a pious Jew, a *hasid*, who added the statements on divine retribution that would be necessary to deal with the prosperity of the wicked. Siegfried also saw five more types of additions to the book.

Rankin indicates two other scholars of critical bent who agree somewhat with Siegfried but also differ. A. H. McNeile, in *An Introduction to Ecclesiastes* (Cambridge: Cambridge University Press [1904]), suggests that Siegfried cut Ecclesiastes up too much with his redactors;

and Barton, in *A Critical and Exegetical Commentary on the Book of Ecclesiastes* (New York: Charles Scribner's Sons [1908]), felt that Siegfried went too far in failing to realize that one author can, under different circumstances, have a variety of conceptions. Yet both of these men did not deviate too far from Siegfried. While they did not see any evidence for any additions by a Hellenistic, religious Jew with an Epicurean slant, they nevertheless agreed that a wisdom writer as well as a pious person did add their comments to an original text.

Rankin has provided charts that list all the passages that each of the three critics assigned to the wisdom and pious writers. While the lists differ among the three, the passages to which all agree concerning the wisdom additions are: 4:5; 7:11–12, 18; 8:1; 9:17–18; 10:3, 12–14, 15. The passages in which there is agreement regarding the pious person's contributions are: 2:26a; 3:17; 7:29; 8:2b–3a, 5–6a, 11–13; 11:9b; 12:1a. Another scholar, E. O. Podechard, in his "La Composition du livre de l'Ecclesiaste" (*Revue Biblique*, IX [1912], pp. 161–91), thought that some beloved disciple of Qohelet added 12:9–12.

In the light of these and many other suggestions about who provided contributions to Ecclesiastes to produce a many-authored book, what happens to the integrity of Ecclesiastes as a single book? The critics assert that an author can produce a piece of literature only with one style of writing. The presence of two or more styles therefore suggests the presence of two or more authors. Is it right to say that each writer can deal only with a single subject, such as that which is pessimistic, cynical, and gloomy, while another author presents that which is positive wisdom and still another deals only with pious statements? Why do we have to follow the assertion of this theory? I was once an engineer who during the day wrote engineering reports complicated with the data of electronics. When away from home on assignments, however, I also wrote notes of endearment to my wife; obviously, the styles of both sets of writings were poles apart! Why cannot one writer or teacher handle different subjects and styles with comparative ease as the occasion and situation demand? We have already seen the many purposes and the theme defined in Ecclesiastes, and almost any godly person of wisdom could say about the same things that the Teacher said hundreds of years ago. It is not inconceivable that a speaker can deal with the gloomy prospects of life but every now and then introduce elements of thought that tend to uplift an audience and even give occasion to chuckle and laugh. Why cannot the Teacher likewise handle gloomy subjects, such as having to face death, and at the same time revive our spirits by telling us to enjoy life, receive it as a gift from God, and then send us into gales of laughter as he talks about the fool who did not even know the way to town (or did not even know enough to come in out of the rain; 10:15)? It seems, therefore, that one man can be responsible for the different facets and viewpoints found in a book such as Ecclesiastes.

The False Claims of Cults

From what is declared in 9:5, "for the living know they will die, but the dead know nothing," some have thought that this statement is an argument for soul sleep. The idea is that when a person dies, his body will decay; but the New Testament speaks of such a person as having fallen asleep. Since he knows nothing, it is felt that his soul has fallen asleep too. Therefore, some people promote the doctrine of soul sleep.

But we have to recognize what the Teacher declares in the context of the passage. He is not stating that those who have left this life are in a state of unconsciousness; all he is saying is that once a person has left the arena of this life and is in the next world, then from that vantage point he does not make decisions any more in this world or make the choices that either will give him a reward or cause him to suffer loss. When a person is in the next world it does not mean that he is unconscious. The Old Testament teaches that a person goes to Sheol after he dies. While the Bible does not state specifically about how a person thinks and expresses himself in the next world, Jesus clearly described what does happen, particularly in the true story of Lazarus and the rich man (Luke 16:19ff.). Both were in specific places, both were conscious, and both were already receiving their rewards in accordance with the choices made while in this life.

It is wrong to read a doctrine into Ecclesiastes that the Teacher does not mean to present. Furthermore, it is a double standard of interpretation to take a doctrine from the New Testament which teaches that a believer, including his soul, falls asleep after death and ignore what it says about how conscious people are after they die. At any rate, we have to be careful that we do not read an entire New Testament revelation into what the Teacher had as his theme and purposes.

Some cults insist that Ecclesiastes does not teach immortality and point to passages such as 3:20, "All go to the same place; all come from dust, and to dust all return." However, to so use this verse is to take it out of its context. The Teacher only declared that someday we will all die and our bodies will return to the ground. But what about the warning as to how we live in this world because we will have to give an account to God *after* we leave this world (12:13–14), clearly an expression of immortality? In what sense do we give an account of ourselves if we no longer exist? Once again we have to keep in mind the Teacher's theme and the purposes of his burden—that we learn how to live wisely in this world. A sound interpretation of the Scriptures insists that we must pull together all of Bible truth in order to get at the total message of God's communication to us. The Old Testament world did not know of annihilation. The dead waited in Sheol to face judgment by God; but when we desire additional information concerning what happens after this life, we go to other portions of Scripture. It is unfair to read the whole Bible into Ecclesiastes to make the Teacher teach everything, and it is certainly wrong to wrench texts out of contexts to teach false doctrine.

Key Words

The key words and phrases in Ecclesiastes are: "under the sun," used thirty-four times; "meaningless," thirty-three times; and the different shades of the word for wisdom (*hokmah, hakam*), used fifty-four times. The key phrase "under the sun" marks the arena of the Teacher's interest where believer and unbeliever live; and his encouragement is to choose wisdom and live wisely so as to give a good account to God.

Ecclesiastes and the Wisdom of the Middle East

The student in a secular university is generally taught that the orderly and formal history of man's rationalizations begins in ancient Greece about the sixth century B.C. with the early Greek philosophers, Thales and others, who sought to understand the world. In no way, however, should we have the idea that this is the first time man began to think or had a peculiar kind of wisdom literature. Solomon, in the 900s B.C., provided a wisdom that came from God and presented a moral to direct man in how to live in this world. Archaeologists have provided research that describes a wisdom literature that can be traced to the earliest historical records of man we have today, 3,500 B.C. in the Tigris-Euphrates Valley and about 3,000 B.C. in Egypt.

The following are examples to show the similarity between some of the statements in Ecclesiastes and the wisdom literature of other Middle Eastern sources:

1. From the Gilgamesh Epic of Old Babylonian literature as provided by Gordis in *Koheleth, The Man and His World* (New York: Schocken Books [1968], p. 54):

> Since the gods created man.
> Death they ordained for man,
> Life in their hands they hold.
> Thou, O Gilgamesh, fill indeed thy belly,
> Day and night be thou joyful.
> Daily ordain gladness,
> Day and night rage and make merry,
> Let thy garments be bright,
> Thy head purify, wash with water,
> Desire thy children which thy hand possesses,
> A wife enjoy in thy bosom,
> Peaceably thy work (?) . . .

One sees a parallel between the Gilgamesh Epic and Ecclesiastes 9:7–10, but there is also an obvious difference between the two. The advice to Gilgamesh consists only of being joyful, raging, and making merry, and enjoying a wife, as if life consists only of seeking pleasure in itself. While the wisdom of Ecclesiastes may sound comparable to the instructions to Gilgamesh, the Teacher advises that the pleasures of life must be enjoyed in moderation and that we will have to give an account for what we do during the days of our lifetime. The difference between the Teacher and the other wisdom literature of the Middle East is the presentation of a moral that comes from God; life can be enjoyed but not in exceeding the moral bounds that a divine King has placed on man.

2. In the Egyptian instruction of the Vizier Ptah-Hotep provided by J. B. Pritchard in *Ancient Near Eastern Texts* (Princeton: Princeton University Press [1955], p. 13):

> If thou are a poor fellow, following a man of distinction, one of good standing with the god, know thou not his former insignificance. Thou shouldst not be puffed-up against him because of what thou didst know of him formerly. Show regard for him in conformance with what has accrued to him—property does not

come of itself. It is their law for him who wishes them. As for him who oversteps, he is feared. It is god who makes (a man's) quality, and he defends him (even) while he is asleep. . . .

The wise advice given to this Vizier is apparently similar to Ecclesiastes 5:18–19. Some have suggested that the Teacher could have borrowed from Egyptian wisdom literature. However, it is not necessary that such an assertion be made because there was and is always the common search by all mankind for the meaning and purpose of life; because of common interests and even common grace, we will see similarities running through all of this wisdom literature. However, when we compare the totality of what Ecclesiastes declares alongside that of the Egyptian wisdom literature, there are major differences that can be attributed only to the wisdom God gave to Solomon the Teacher in the special sense in which he had it.

3. From the same instructions to Ptah-Hotep:

As for the fool who does not hearken, *he cannot do anything.* He regards knowledge as ignorance and profit as loss. He does everything blameworthy, so that one finds fault with him every day. He lives on that through which he should die, and guilt is his food. His character therefrom is told as something known to the officials: dying while alive every day. . . .

Once again we see another similarity, this time with Ecclesiastes 10:12–15, particularly the line in verse 15 which indicates that the fool "does not know the way to town." One cannot help but realize the common concern of all peoples to avoid the folly of the fool.

4. In the instruction to Ptah-Hotep is the description of the infirmities of old age:

O sovereign, my lord! Oldness has come; old age has descended. Feebleness has arrived; dotage is coming anew. The heart sleeps wearily every day. The eyes are weak, the ears are deaf, the strength is disappearing because of weariness of heart, and the mouth is silent and cannot speak. The heart is forgetful and cannot recall yesterday. The bone suffers old age. Good is become evil. All taste is gone. What old age does to men is evil in every respect. The nose is stopped up and cannot breathe. (Simply) to stand up or to sit down is difficult.

Other peoples besides those in Israel had a dismal report about what happens to a person in old age, even as the Teacher described it (12:2–7). Nevertheless, Ecclesiastes has a basic difference in that the young person is warned before he reaches old age so that he will put God in the center of his life since he is accountable for what he does in this world.

Therefore, we see similarities concerning life in wisdom literature of all the peoples of the Middle East; but there are different vantage points. The wisdom literature of Israel reflects the revelation of God that was given to His people and, in particular, to Solomon who had a wisdom that made him the most famous in his day (1 Kings 10:1–7).

Outline

Ecclesiastes has been outlined in many different ways by commentators. However, it is not difficult to recognize certain divisions: the prologue (1:1–11); the search for some kind of meaning to life in examining the different facets of it (1:12–2:26); the change in subject matter in chapter 3, which begins with a discussion concerning the most appropriate times that certain events occur; and finally the epilogue (12:9–14), which is the Teacher's conclusion. There is a certain order in the progression of the thought of the Teacher although there might appear to be digressions from the main thought. But what preacher does not digress in his message, sometimes as a calculated device to keep us interested?

The outline below represents an honest attempt on my part to get at what the Teacher had in mind: the search for meaning (1:12–2:26); the search for reality in life's pursuits (3:1–6:12); and then the many-faceted wise advice on how to cope with this life (7:1–12:8). While other authors see a break in thought between 8:16 or 17 and 9:1–12:8, it seems to me that the Teacher was continuing his discussion of how to face and cope with the different problems of life.

Chapter 1: Prologue (1:1–11)
    A. The Author (1:1)
    B. One Basic Conclusion of Life (1:2)
    C. Round and Round We Go (1:3–11)
Chapter 2: The Search for Meaning in Wisdom, Pleasures, and Materialism (1:12–2:26)
    A. In Pursuit of Wisdom Alone (1:2–18)

For Further Study

1. From the bibliography, list opinions of how different commentators regard the wisdom of the Old Testament wisdom books.

2. Can you also see the purposes of Ecclesiastes in men such as Moses, David, or Daniel? How?

3. Because of the theme assigned to Ecclesiastes by the author, could some philosophers with their philosophical systems still accuse the Christian of giving up too easily on the pursuit of knowledge? Why or why not? Could we charge that philosophers also fall short of what can be learned in this world? In other words, do some philosophers intentionally lock out areas of knowledge that can be known, as for example, the naturalists who do not accept the premise that there is a supreme being?

4. Research the term *qohelet* in the lexicons.

5. Research the debate between the houses of Shammai and Hillel concerning how Ecclesiastes was finally accepted into the canon. You can start with Megilla 7a in Moed, IV, pp. 35–37 and Shabbath 30 in Moed, I, pp. 131–38, *The Babylonian Talmud* (London: The Soncino Press [1938]).

6. Using books listed in the bibliography, research and list pro and con the various suggestions as to who the author of Ecclesiastes might be.

7. Research from the commentaries the different suggestions as to when in his life Solomon could have written Ecclesiastes.

8. Research what other conservative writers have to say about how a single author can use two different styles of writing under different circumstances. See O. T. Allis, *The Five Books of Moses* (Philadelphia: Presbyterian and Reformed Publishing Co. [1964], pp. 40ff.) to begin.

9. Research the doctrine of soul sleep.

Abbreviations

BDB   Brown-Driver-Briggs, eds., *Hebrew and English Lexicon of the Old Testament* (Oxford: Clarendon Press [1968], reprint).

Cohen   A. Cohen and V. Reichert, eds., "Ecclesiastes," *The Five Megillot* (London: The Socino Press [1952]).

Delitzsch   F. Delitzsch, "Song of Songs and Ecclesiastes," *Commentaries on the Old Testament* (Grand Rapids: Eerdmans [1950]).

Genung   John F. Genung, *Words of Koheleth* (New York: Houghton, Mifflin [1904]).

Ginsburg   David Christian Ginsburg, *The Song of Songs and Coheleth* (New York: KTAV [1970]).

Gordis   Robert Gordis, *Koheleth, The Man and His World* (New York: Schocken [1968]).

Leupold   H. C. Leupold, *Exposition of Ecclesiastes* (Grand Rapids: Baker [1952]).

Chapter 1

Prologue
(Ecclesiastes 1:1–11)

A. The Author (1:1)

The author has already been identified; he is the son of David, king in Jerusalem, marking him as Solomon. He has taken the title of Teacher *(qohelet)* inasmuch as he is relating his experiences of life for the benefit of other people and for the many who will follow him.

The English title of the book, Ecclesiastes, comes from the Septuagint; but the Hebrew title, the Teacher *(qohelet),* is more descriptive. The Hebrew root of *qohelet* is *qahal* which means to gather as in a public assembly. Therefore, *qohelet* can mean "Teacher" or "Preacher," one who addresses a public assembly or one who is a collector (of sayings) (BDB, p. 875).

B. One Basic Conclusion of Life (1:2)

Every teacher and preacher has his introduction. There are short introductions while others take up almost the whole message. Solomon has a very terse statement, "Meaningless! Meaningless! . . . Everything is meaningless."

As already seen, this word *(hevel)* is used thirty-three times in the book. Its basic meaning is "vapor" or "breath" (BDB, p. 210) and can be described by what occurs when one exhales into winter air. The breath appears to condense and then disappears altogether. Therefore, the word picture means something that is fleeting and only transitory, hence "vanity" or "meaningless."

Although the NIV renders *hevel* as "meaningless," "without meaning" in every instance, the Hebrew word can lend itself to other shades of meaning, depending on the context. For example, in 8:14 we could say that it is senseless when the righteous get what the wicked deserve and the wicked receive what the righteous deserve. The Teacher adds for emphasis in the verse that this is senseless. Or, in 11:10, we could indicate that youth and vigor are fleeting. Therefore, we need to have a sense for the context that can bring out various shades of understanding man's experiences in this world where many situations are less than desirable.

It is not the Teacher's understanding that *all* of life is empty and completely without meaning. We have already pointed out in the Introduction that there are areas of life that can be enjoyed, and to become totally immersed in any one pursuit of interest can lead to serious consequences. The Teacher wants to give us a balanced view of life and not lead us into the swamp of pessimism that is not warranted by the totality of his experiences and the message based on them. By no means do we want to accuse God of the fact that His world is completely meaningless in the sense that there is nothing good in it. The Teacher does stress that there are good things in life also. In the Book of Ecclesiastes we are reminded of how earthly things pass away, how so many experiences seem senseless and questionable; and therefore we are not to trust with complete confidence in what goes on in this world.

The phrase "utterly meaningless!" is the Hebrew superlative for emphasis, meaningless of meaninglesses. This phenomenon occurs many times elsewhere; for example, Song of Songs (Song 1:1) and holy of holies (Exod. 26:33–34 NASB). In English, the idea of 1:2b is, "Oh, how utterly meaningless, how utterly meaningless are all things." We might ask, "What is utterly meaningless?" But the Teacher takes his time and explores a number of areas of life that we can see and experience for ourselves. In the end we will nod our heads in approval because most human beings, no matter where they live, have the same basic problems as they contemplate life. But where many people become completely pessimistic with life and want to give up on it, the Teacher in the end is revealed as a man of faith. He wants to share with us his understanding so that we also can live the best possible kind of life.

C. Round and Round We Go (1:3–11)

Before plunging into the many experiences of the Teacher, we obtain a bearing on what he will say as he introduces the subject of his experiences. In verse 3 he asks, "What does man gain from all his labor?" The word "gain" *(yitron),* translated also as profit and advantage, has the basic idea of a commercial term and therefore refers to wage or reward or what is left over when a business venture is completed. But the context is much wider than mere business; the Teacher is talking about all the labor at which a person toils under the sun. (See Genung, *Words of Koheleth*, pp. 214–15). One must not become downhearted and pessimistic and answer, "Nothing!" This can only lead to extreme cynicism and is not warranted by what will be said in the rest of the book, or the rest of Scripture for that matter.

We cannot forget that God created the world and pronounced it as very good (Gen. 1:31). But there was also the calamity of the Fall that affected the world in which we live, especially man himself. As a result, the phrase "under the sun" becomes one key of the book. Man has to realize that all that is accomplished in this world apart from any understanding of God can become meaningless and transitory. If all we live for in this world is "under the sun," then we shall find that our involvement with it is fleeting indeed. The Teacher felt that this phrase, "under the sun," is so important that he repeated it thirty-four times to remind us that we are two-dimensional creatures—horizontal as we face this world and vertical as we face God.

However, as we have indicated already, no portion of this book can be taken out of the context of the whole message. No one should help himself to verse 3, wrench it from the total message, and then say that the Teacher is a pessimist. He certainly hedges himself in his total message with the acknowledgment that God of necessity must be in the center of his world.

In the rest of the prologue he looks at four examples to substantiate his opening statements concerning meaninglessness and what gain there is under the sun for all his labors. There are people who feel that they can make this world a better place and have strong motivation to leave something better for generations to come. Edison, for example, relieved many of man's labors through the application of what electricity can do. Lincoln tried to relieve so much of man's misery. Yet even an Edison and a Lincoln passed off this earth's scene as will the rest of us. The Teacher emphasizes how generations come and go, how most people are soon forgotten by following generations. This earth will see the last of our generation off its scene, and then what will be the meaning of most of our striving (v. 4)? Only the earth remains since it is more permanent than mankind.

The Teacher also points out that there is a ceaseless and changeless cycle about the world's own pattern (v. 5). The sun rises and then sets, and it hastens (literally, pants) with eagerness to return to its place from where it will rise again. It is not the sun, however, that is a figure of the vanity of life with its monotonous repetition of motion. The sun is an object planned by God for the good of man, providing for the growth of food and for light and heat by which man can work and warm himself. But the Teacher refers to the ceaseless round of rising, setting, and then returning to the starting point, an activity that appears more constant than the fleeting presence of man.

Another example is the wind (v. 6). While the sun generally has an east-west motion, the wind is seen as blowing to the south and then returning to the north, thereby including the four directions of the compass and everything in between. As we look at the weather maps today, we observe this phenomenon of winds revolving around high and low pressures that bring us either good or bad weather. The movement of the wind by itself represents an ever continuing sequence, but man again by comparison is transitory.

The last example describes the round of nature as seen in the flow of waters in their channels (v. 7). The streams are observed to flow into the sea, but the sea is never full. It appeared that waters from the sea did return to the place where they originally started at the headwaters of the streams. The point is not to assign to the Teacher all the latest knowledge of meteorology as to how the waters in the rivers flow into the sea; the process whereby the sun evaporates the water so that the latter becomes a vapor; how the vapor, when moving across land again under the right atmospheric conditions, condenses so as to fall in the form of snow or rain; and how the process repeats itself so that the waters run into the sea again. All of these facts were not in the thinking of the Teacher; but rather, the unwearied process of the rivers running into the seas merely reflects a process that keeps repeating itself. Once again it is man who is transitory in comparison with the repetitious sequences one can observe on earth.

The unending repetition of the things of this world can be quite wearisome (v. 8). All the processes, sequences, etc., of this world in unending repetition seem to give the impression of weariness and fatigue. And if man is living for this world only, continually observing all that goes on, his eyes will never observe it all and his ears will never have their fill of hearing. The unrest of the processes of this world also will reflect themselves in the inner man.

The eyes have lost their anticipation of seeing another thing, and the ears simply do not wish to hear another story or account. All life becomes monotonous; what has been done will be repeated and what has been already will be once again (v. 9). The Teacher concludes that there is nothing new under the sun. But why does he make such a statement? Does there not appear from time to time something that we can call new? Not really. We are not talking here about new inventions, and we need to recognize that man is quite inventive. Rather, the Teacher has in mind the round of life and what people might call new in it, this round has existed in one form or another long ago in a previous generation (v. 10).

In verse 11 we have to agree with the basic argumentation of the Teacher: man has a short memory. In reflection on 1:3–4, we know so little of the *men* who lived in previous generations; and future generations will not remember our *children*. Therefore, man is transient while nature and its processes go on and on. Others, however, want to connect verses 10 and 11 to indicate that the reason there is nothing new is that we have no remembrance of earlier *things* and future generations will not remember the later *things* that occur (H. C. Leupold, *Exposition of Ecclesiastes*, p. 49). But regardless of the two views, the end result is still the same: From one generation to the next, man does not remember.

Once again we must insist that the Teacher was not a pessimist giving vent to a howl of lament. He had learned in the experiences of life that if we live only for earthly values, then what will be the meaning of our fleeting presence as contrasted with the endless existence of the earth and the continuing processes of the natural phenomena of sun, wind, and water? At least he raised the right questions in verse 3 as to what gain there is if we live for this world only. But contrary to the pessimist, he is not through with his search even though the view might seem to be bleak up to now. Don't write man off yet!

We need to make one more observation. It has already been indicated that the Teacher's basic source of authority is a wisdom provided by God. But there are some who see a link between what the Teacher is saying and Greek influence, particularly the Stoics who had the view that all eternal existence repeats itself in the same pattern again and again in predetermined intervals. The future, therefore, consists of a fixed, repetitive experience where everything in the universe comes around again to the context in which we find ourselves.

There seems to be similarity, particularly from what we have seen in 1:9, "What has been will be again." But similarities do not necessarily prove dependence. The Teacher does not subscribe to the Stoic view. In one sense of this view, if all processes are fixed, then how can man exercise his moral choices and affect the way he lives? The Teacher eventually declares that the moral choices of individuals do mean something and that there also will be a judgment that will change the present course of things. The biblical view is that the processes of this world will not go on and on indefinitely, but man can change the outward course of things by his choices for proper behavior. Rather, the seeming description of how the processes of nature repeat themselves is only to highlight how transitory man really is.

For Further Study

1. Look up in a Bible dictionary the meaning and many usages of *hevel*, meaningless (vanity KJV).

2. Why does the phrase "under the sun" become so important for the Teacher? Does this phrase have only one consideration or emphasis?

3. Discuss the Teacher's four examples in trying to arrive at an understanding of "What does man gain from all his labor . . . under the sun?"

4. Discuss several areas that offer a contrast to a seeming pessimism.

Chapter 2

The Search for Meaning in Wisdom, Pleasures, and Materialism
(Ecclesiastes 1:12–2:26)

Once again the Teacher announces his identity as king over Israel in Jerusalem (1:12). This time he has switched from the third person with which he started in 1:1 to first person. It is as if he is going to make the point that he himself was personally involved in the search for meaning in life. After a lifetime in pursuit of a wide range of interests, he now wants to inform his audience of his experiences and conclusions. Up to this point he has been speaking only in generalities concerning the unending round of some of earth's phenomena; there did not seem to be any answer to why man struggles and seems to gain nothing for all his efforts. But now he wants to talk about specific pursuits as he sought basic answers to life's problems.

A. In Pursuit of Wisdom Alone (1:12–18)

One area of interest was wisdom. As already indicated, Israel had a wisdom distinctive from the Greek speculative kind. Solomon was responsible for much of the Book of Proverbs; and because of his expertise in wisdom, his fame spread far and wide, among Israel and non-Jewish peoples. This was the attraction that brought the Queen of Sheba to his court.

The Teacher begins with a summation statement concerning the proper place of wisdom in the pursuits among men (v. 13). He had given his whole heart, all his mental faculties, to acquire wisdom in as wide an area as possible. He studied or searched the very roots of each area of investigation and explored every subject from all sides. With what he knew he tried to analyze well the facts of a subject. But he sums up his search with a disheartening statement, "a heavy (sorry)

43

burden," suggesting that this entire business can drive a person to despair.

What is puzzling is the statement by the Teacher, after decrying the search for truth by wisdom, that God Himself gave this task to man. Why did God do so? It is here that we need to remember that God created man with a moral nature, with the ability to *know* right and wrong. In spite of the Fall, man still has the glimmer of moral values even though he does not live up to what he knows. But man also has the urge, given by God as well, to discover truth; by no means is this limited to believers only. Many, even those who do not know the Lord, have an inner compulsion to seek out truth. Yet at the same time, the more a man strives to know the world around him, the more he fails to achieve his goal of complete satisfaction. We shall say more about the reasons for failure at the end of this section.

The final goal of the study of all things under heaven (v. 13), a phrase similar to "under the sun," is meaningless and actually "chasing after the wind" (v. 14). It does not matter how extensive a research of an area is under investigation. The results of the search leaves much to be desired because there will always be the frustration of so many situations. We have to ask, "Does all this information really change things? Do we really straighten out what is twisted? Because so many of life's circumstances seem so hopeless, can we even begin to count what is lacking?" This world has so many unanswered problems; and with the wisdom we have, we cannot, in many situations, even begin to provide answers. By no means is the Teacher saying that we should not try to help and rectify specific hurts, inequities, needs, etc.; but all the wisdom he had acquired is not able to solve all the world's problems.

The Teacher continues with his thoughts in reflection (1:16–17). There is no doubt that Solomon was an eminent and very wise person. He had succeeded in becoming a great man inasmuch as he had access to resources others did not have. He had grown in wisdom more than those who preceded him and, it is safe to say, more than most who followed him. He had added to the wisdom God gave him so that his accumulation of wisdom and knowledge was great. He was thorough in every area he sought out, and his search was a noble exercise. Somehow he also sought for what knowledge could be obtained in frivolity (v. 17), but this is an area that we will discuss in the next section.

What is the conclusion in seeking for wisdom and knowledge "under the sun," that is, a wisdom without the element of the divine in the center of it? With a woeful sigh, the Teacher calls this kind of a search a "chasing after the wind." The effort for wisdom, as great as it can be, only produces little of lasting value. But some will ask, "What is the point of obtaining an education if in the end all such efforts bring meager results?" Some will say that we have a much better life to enjoy because of all the research in applied science. We enjoy all the gadgets of modern life, such as cars, refrigeration, washing machines, and stereos. So why does the Teacher adopt so pessimistic an attitude about wisdom and knowledge and refer to it as mere wind?

Perhaps we might see two areas in which the author's complaint is valid. If wisdom and knowledge are all a man lives for, then life can become empty. If a person spends all his time, as Solomon probably did at one point, in studying all there is to know about botany (e.g., from the cedar of Lebanon to the little sprig of hyssop and everything in between, 1 Kings 4:33), biology and zoology (animals, birds, reptiles, and fish), and indeed all the subjects of academic discipline, what will all this endeavor mean in the long run? If a person becomes a professional scholar and lives only for his study, how will he be able to relate to the rest of life? The Teacher could take only a dim view of a situation where learning is all there is to life. In the long run, such a context is "chasing the wind."

Whether Solomon was talking about philosophic thought is extremely doubtful. He lived in a society that had a revelation from God. Even though the Teacher did backslide for a good portion of his life (1 Kings 11), yet he knew better than to deal with knowledge as the Greeks did. There is no evidence in the book that the author has in mind the processes of thought such as espoused by Plato and Aristotle. But the principles that Solomon did derive from his pursuit of wisdom and knowledge can be apropos for one involved in rational processes.

Still another problem remains. Even with the access to the revelation of God, what happens when a person lives only for intellectual pursuits? As he learns more and more, he will discover that the horizons of knowledge are ever extended. The progression in knowledge only makes one realize that he really knows very little in comparison to the increase of comprehension that there is still much more that needs to be learned. Where is the end of it all if this is all a person lives for? It is no wonder that the Teacher exclaimed in a proverb that with "much wisdom comes much sorrow" (irritation) and that with the increase in knowledge there is also an increase in grief or pain (1:18). He realized that one will never learn it all.

One also must understand that with the greater knowledge we obtain with diligent search, we can only admit that there are many things that are wrong in this world and that can never be straightened out. Do we become pessimistic, therefore, and cry out as the Teacher did, "What profit is there?" (1:3) Wisdom and knowledge have to be put into perspective and a balance needs to be maintained; we cannot live only for storing up knowledge. God has to be in the center of all that we do, a refrain that is repeated throughout this book. We can take some comfort from the fact that God knows the situation here on earth and that some day all will be rectified.

B. Pleasure to the Fullest (2:1–3)

Another interest occupied the Teacher's attention: the enjoyment of pleasure. During one period of his life he pursued and attempted to extract from life all the pleasures it afforded. There is no doubt that the Solomonic era was one period in Jewish history when it was possible to enter into various pleasures because of the wealth at hand to pay for every indulgence. And the king was in a better position than most to take advantage of every possibility. Will these interests demonstrate the advantage for which the Teacher was seeking?

There were at least four ways by which the Teacher sought to satisfy his fleshly desires. The first mentioned and quite prominent indulgence is pleasure, and he desired to test himself to see what was good. The word for pleasure (simḥah) can take on in this context the involvement with amusements and delights of life that make a person happy. If his daily provisions were "thirty cors of fine flour and sixty cors of meal, ten head of stall-fed cattle, twenty of pasture-fed cattle and a hundred sheep and goats, as well as deer, gazelles, roebucks and choice fowl" (1 Kings 4:22–23), then we can imagine what some of his pleasures entailed—it meant chefs and gourmet cooking, and elaborate furnishings to enhance his tables and to entertain his guests. It was an endless round.

One writer describes this situation, "He amused himself with a lot of fun." But in the end, after the Teacher had recovered his bearings in life, what was his assessment of the round of eating and drinking? Why, it simply had no lasting value. After all, what does pleasure accomplish? If we live only for fun and food, where will we find meaning?

When the hard tests in life come, how will we comfort someone who needs help for his grief? The Teacher's experiment applies for our day as well.

Still another dimension of the so-called pleasures of life is laughter (v. 2). There is nothing wrong with a good sense of humor, but the Teacher was thinking of much more. He turned his life into a round of clowning and laughter. One can imagine the endless procession of court jesters and comedians frequenting the palace and making fun at the banquet tables. This was not innocent humor because many times in Scripture we read that laughter and madness went hand in hand with evil (see 9:3 and 10:13), even as the Teacher admitted. The laughter had immoral overtones which, in the end, led to evil foolishness in the many pursuits of pleasure. Eventually, Solomon pronounced laughter as sheer madness. After being involved in such a round of humor, we might well ask when we are quiet and alone, "What was so funny?" Almost half of our television programs are comedies that might be all right for an occasional outlet for emotions, but much of what passes for comedy and jokes is in reality sick, and it does not help those who need something more basic in life to help them in their sorrows.

The Teacher mentions another so-called good thing of life: wine (v. 3). In this respect he does not mean debauchery because he involves the use of his mind to guide him. He probably is thinking of being a connoisseur in selecting the right kinds of wine that go with the best food at the lavish banquets he gave in abundance. With his wisdom guiding him, he experimented with the proper balance of wine and folly to try to find the perfect combination of amusement that was a part of the enjoyment of a banquet. He wanted to try out this lifestyle, and he had all the adequate means to do so. But in the end, what did all this eating and drinking amount to?

A final area of pursuit needs to be mentioned. Solomon's interest in women reached the point where he had 700 wives and 300 concubines (1 Kings 11:3). Many of the wives were acquired, no doubt, in the ratification of commercial trade treaties that Solomon made with numerous traders who represented many kings. This arrangement made it convenient for a king to either show a deep-seated interest in the treaty by giving away a daughter, or gave him a convenient way to get rid of a daughter for whom no suitable husband could be found. Whatever the reason, Solomon had plenty of opportunities to be extremely interested in and amused with his many women.

So dangerous did this "fun" become that the love for many pagan women actually turned Solomon's heart away from the Lord, and he followed other gods and built pagan shrines for his wives (1 Kings 11:3, 4). It probably was not until he was beyond this interest that he realized he was not accomplishing anything. The truth is no less important today. Many in our age try to satisfy their lives with one woman after another, only to discover that this attempt is not really love but only meaninglessness.

In the end, what does pleasure to the fullest amount to? There is almost a note of pathos in this pursuit as Solomon talked about what was done under heaven in the few days of men's lives. How many banquets can we go to, sampling all the varieties of wines and delicious food, and how much experimenting with sex do we have to engage in before asking, "Is this really living?" or "What does it profit?" It is a delight once in a while to get away, partake of good food, and relax, especially after working hard. But to engage in constant eating at banquets can become quite meaningless. Obviously, man needs something more meaningful in life.

C. Material Things Without End (2:4–11)

During one period of Solomon's life he gave himself to the acquisition of material possessions and was involved in substantial building projects. While he no doubt had the best interests of the nation at heart, there is every reason to believe that he also sought personal satisfaction with what can be found in "things." Again, Solomon was the one who was best suited for this kind of interest, and the times in which he lived made it conducive for him to do so (1 Kings 4:21–23).

The Teacher first mentions houses and vineyards (v. 4). The most important of his building operations was the first temple that bore his name. David had amassed many materials for the temple, but God had told him that his son would complete the project (1 Chron. 22:1–10). Within four years after David's death, Solomon began this most important project. It took seven years (1 Kings 6:1, 38) and was to serve Israel as its spiritual center.

But this was only the beginning. He built a palace for himself which took thirteen years and the Palace of the Forest of Lebanon (1 Kings 7:1–2; 9:10; 10:17). He built still another building which was for his wife, the daughter of a pharaoh (1 Kings 7:8). Solomon had store cities (2 Chron. 8:1–6) and fortified areas—Millo (the fortified line between the temple mount and the city of David just south of it), the wall of Jerusalem, and the military cities of Hazor, Megiddo, and Gezer. Hazor was in the northern part of Israel, standing in a sense at the gateway leading to the valley of Esdraelon. At the south end of this valley there is a road linking Damascus and Egypt, running east-west across this part of the country. At the Mediterranean seacoast the road turns south to Egypt. Obviously this valley was strategic; Megiddo, at one point in the valley, became the second line of defense in the event Hazor would ever fall in an attack from the north. Both Hazor and Megiddo have been excavated in recent years; and the results of the finds are quite interesting, particularly that which relates to Solomonic influence.

Vineyards are also mentioned. There is no reference to Solomon's vineyards in the historical books of Kings and Chronicles although one is mentioned in the Song of Songs (8:11). David did have them, and these no doubt passed to Solomon (1 Chron. 27:27), who probably expanded them.

The Teacher also talked of his gardens and parks that had all kinds of fruit trees (v. 5). In a sense we could say he was involved in horticulture although no indication of this is preserved in the historical narratives. The land of Israel is conducive for growing fruit trees as evidenced today. Perhaps Solomon experimented with what different kinds could be grown, a factor that could enhance the economy of the country. The word for parks is a Persian loan-word meaning enclosure and would aptly describe the area set aside. The word has passed into Greek as *paradeisos* and comes through in English as paradise.

Still another project closely connected with verse 5 is the work Solomon engaged in for the construction of reservoirs to irrigate groves of trees (v. 6). The mention of water and irrigation certainly conjures up deep concern in Israel today where such commodities are precious and these were essential in the buildup of the state. The problem was no less acute in ancient days, and Jerusalem has always been notorious for its lack of water. Collecting water was extremely necessary, and we read in the Song of Songs 7:4 of a reference to the pools of Heshbon. Today, just south of Bethlehem, there are large pools for collecting water referred to as the "Pools of Solomon." There is no doubt, however, that these reservoirs were a project of Roman times although they could have been rebuilt due to an earlier effort by Solomon. If this was the area for the pools, it was then a marvelous engineering feat, because the piping to Jerusalem is based on a gravity feed, meaning the pipes follow a path around the hills leading into Jerusalem. The road from Jerusalem to the pools is just under fourteen miles, but the length of the pipes to effect this gravity feed stretches about thirty-four miles!

This water was needed for a grove of trees as well as the parks. The ancient situation of a land of trees was not to be seen in the early 1900s. Israelis today have been patiently planting trees all over the land of Israel, but to have what Solomon describes was a special effort among the many forests in Israel at that time. The Teacher was not referring to an afforestation project but rather to a private effort for his own delight. The emphasis on a personal project is seen in the phrase "for myself," which is repeated a number of times in this passage alone.

In order to handle all his projects and run his palace, it was necessary for Solomon to have a large number of servants (v. 7). He bought all kinds of slaves for his many needs, both male and female. He also had slaves who were born on his own establishments and would be loyal to their master.

In no way is this practice to be construed as a rationale for slavery. While extreme care was taken in the Mosaic constitution so as not to upset the economic fabric of society by calling for a release of all slaves at one time, an acquired slave had to serve for only six years; in the seventh year he was given the privilege of freedom (Exod. 21:2). With the ancient world as a background, and not judging the situation from present conditions, the idea of freeing slaves in accordance with the Law was a revolutionary concept. Yet in Solomon's context, the servants ran the household and did much of the work on his projects.

One special interest was the maintaining of large herds of cattle and flocks of sheep and goats. Some of these would of necessity be used for the many sacrifices. In particular, the king offered 22,000 oxen and 120,000 sheep when the temple was dedicated. This amount of livestock required many servants as caretakers and is an indication of the extent of Solomon's livestock because the number sacrificed was only a portion of the entire stock. At the same time, the Teacher no doubt also had prize livestock, the best in all Israel; and he had every reason to be proud of them as he relished the memory of these interests.

He quickly mentions other items that were so important to him at one time. Silver and gold he had in abundance (v. 8), and they were as plentiful in Jerusalem as stones (2 Chron. 1:15; 9:27; 1 Kings 10:27), an apt comparison because stones are everywhere in Israel. In addition, the king had ships along with those of the Phoenicians in the Mediterranean. Every three years they sailed to Tarshish and brought back gold, silver, ivory, apes, and baboons (1 Kings 10:22). Solomon's fame in this way spread far and wide among many kings, and he had a reputation among other known nations of the earth.

The reference to singers gives insight to the Teacher's reputation as a patron of the arts. A royal court that would suit the tastes of a monarch such as Solomon definitely required the staging of concerts and musical plays, especially when we realize that the king himself was a musician, writing 1,005 songs (1 Kings 4:32). One could wish to have the many scores of music that the Temple court and royal court orchestras played and that the singers sang. Today in Israel the Israel Philharmonic Orchestra gives more concerts per season than any other orchestra in the world. If this is any gauge of affinity for music, the ancient situation would have been no different.

The reference to a "harem . . . the delights of the heart of man" has posed a problem in understanding the Hebrew word for harem (*shidah veshidot*) and providing its translation. But in J. B. Pritchard's *Ancient Near Eastern Texts*, p. 487a, there is a letter from an Egyptian pharaoh in which he requests forty *concubines,* which is explained by a Canaanite term similar to the words in the Hebrew text here. We suggest the meaning that Solomon had the delights of men, "of mistresses a goodly number," a good correspondence to what is described in 1 Kings 11:1–3. The Teacher admits that he was involved with the very unwise practice of an unbridled sensualism in one period of his life.

We have not tried to describe all the material possessions of Solomon; the reader is referred to 1 Kings 10 and 11 and 2 Chronicles 8 and 9. But he summarizes his impassioned quest for material possessions and things of this world by saying, "I became greater by far than anyone in Jerusalem before me" (v. 9). Of all the kings of Israel, none surpassed him for greatness, wealth, and splendor. Yet at the same time, while in full pursuit of his projects, he kept a scrutinizing eye on all he did because his wisdom remained with him. The God-given wisdom (1 Kings 3:12) did not depart while he gave himself utterly to his acquisition of riches. There is a force in the Hebrew for "I became greater" that literally means "I was great and I added."

Solomon's achievements were brilliant. Whatever he wished for was fulfilled by his command (v. 10). His ambitions had been realized, and he was able to look with pleasure on all he had accomplished. He had realized his deepest desires to be the best builder, the best horticulturalist, the best connoisseur of the arts, and the best purveyor of the aesthetic. He was proud of all he had accomplished, and he did not have to be sad because of unrealized dreams and ambitions; instead, he had an immense amount of pleasure and pride in his work.

At least he thought so while pursuing his objectives. But after it was all over, what then (v. 11)? He found that to be merely involved in things will in the end leave a sense of emptiness in the heart. Like his search for knowledge and reveling in pleasures, the Teacher ruefully had to conclude that there was really more to life than mere things. So after surveying all efforts in this particular area, he had to conclude, "Everything was meaningless, . . . nothing was gained under the sun." In fact, insofar as ultimate issues were concerned, all his efforts were "chasing after the wind." We must learn this lesson too. Pure material possessions can be a disappointment if we are looking for real values.

D. Trying to Find a Balance (2:12–17)

The Teacher now "turned" (v. 12), meaning he wants to discuss something else but not something entirely different. He had given his verdict on wisdom and knowledge (1:17–18), on pleasures (2:1–3), and on material possessions (2:11). Now he wants to assess these areas in relation to one another.

He raises the issue of what would happen if a successor, either a king or another individual, tried to cope with the same problems he had coped with. There can be the danger that men will not handle every angle of the relationship of wisdom, pleasure, and material possessions, pursuits that are of perennial interest from generation to generation. But the Teacher wants to thoroughly discuss these issues and leave no stone unturned as to their implications. In that way, he felt that his experiences would be on record as a warning to posterity where many will not face up to the consequences of wrong choices. The Teacher wants his successors to know what God considers the best possible life a person can live in the here and now and he warns them of the pitfalls.

Wisdom is declared to have its advantages (v. 13). The Teacher does not rule out completely the wisdom that God provides because he benefited greatly from it during his many pursuits in life. It was a wisdom based on the word of God which is the source of a sanctified common sense. A desire to be guided by this kind of wisdom is better than folly, even as "light is better than darkness." After all, a person who justifies the wicked and condemns the righteous is acting the part of the fool (Prov. 17:15). Even many an unregenerate person would consider this state of affairs morally lacking, but the person who is grounded in the Word of God realizes that the wisdom of revelation does not sanction such a topsy-turvy world of values. Neither did the Teacher!

In fact, the one who makes use of this wisdom "has eyes in his head," a good way of describing a person's unfaltering walk in this world (v. 14a). But pity the poor fool who tries to live without the wisdom God provides in His Word. He is regarded as walking in pitch darkness, stumbling across everything in his path (10:15b). From what we have seen concerning folly and its pleasures and piling up a lot of "things," Solomon learned that these were indeed a poor guide for life. At least wisdom can provide the means for the best possible guidance as long as it too is kept in proper perspective.

But now comes the jarring note: the end of all things (v. 14b). Let us not assume that the Teacher was a pessimist. Rather, as we have pointed out already, he was a realist and had lived long enough to face consequences squarely and give us sound advice based on his many experiences. So the Teacher declares what many have already indicated, but he makes his comment with a kind of force, "But I came to realize" that one fate or lot overtakes both wise man and fool in the end. The sobering point is that no matter who the person may be in this life, either wise or fool, he will die (v. 15). Death comes as relentless as taxes; and even though a person may be as wise as Solomon, he also will die at some appointed time.

So what is the point of being wise, of having so much knowledge? Even avoiding a life where all one lives for is the search for further wisdom and knowledge, what did the Teacher gain in trying to know more than others if in the end he would die? The same conclusion comes, "This too is meaningless," that is, how much good is there in having so much wisdom?

As the Teacher was not pessimistic, neither was he a fatalist. Solomon had asked for wisdom at the beginning of his reign (1 Kings 3:9), and God gave it to him; but it was not for the purpose of escaping death. God permits the wise person to die even as the fool, and only in this respect does wisdom become meaningless. He is not fatalistic here, but was merely recognizing the round of life as the arena where wisdom is used. From the point of view of this life, the use of wisdom does not matter any more when death comes.

The Teacher moves us along with his logic. Not only does the wise man die along with the fool, but they both will be forgotten (v. 16). How unfair! Perhaps human achievements can have some lasting value, and a wise person can have the plaudits of his generation. Certainly people should remember him and not the fool who did nothing. But what do we realize? The Teacher has no illusions; after several generations, who remembers the wise man for his accomplishments? We are speaking in generalities, of course, from the point of view of this world; but the Teacher's pronouncements have much too much truth. We cannot brush them aside in spite of what people say. For a few, the memory of the righteous is blessed (Prov. 10:7); but how the generations pass where people in general do not remember those who did much for their specific generation.

The conclusion is now drawn: "So I hated life" (v. 17). For a person of this world as Solomon, who labored so much in many areas and who tasted life for all its pleasures, will react to this conclusion. There will be a few people who will be satisfied with their work and have no regrets with what they accomplished. For the most part, however, we will be unhappy with the Teacher's conclusion.

If a wise king like Solomon, or any other great benefactor, can end up as any fool when both alike die, then the seeming injustice is just too much to take. Too often we see this experience when people on the verge of death give vent to uncontrolled anger as they contemplate their lives. Yet the Teacher did have a greater hope to fall back on when he eventually talked about God and eternity (12:13–14 and 3:11). He was not entirely devoid of faith, but he did express his discontent with the seeming meaninglessness of life when it has to end as it does—and we do the same at times. All his toil for wisdom, therefore, does not appear to have an ultimate advantage.

E. Despair (2:18–23)

Yet another jarring note comes as the Teacher continues to reflect. He had labored long and hard in a number of areas, accomplishing much. He could scarcely accept the fact that in the end he would die just as the fool would die. But who will be the one to inherit all his accomplishments (v. 18)? It is one thing to enjoy the fruit of one's labor in this life, but it is especially distressing to know that all the accomplishments and inheritance will fall into the wrong hands. This situation is not true in every case, but all too often this outcome can be observed. Perhaps Solomon thought of his own successor, Rehoboam, and could have had a lot of apprehension.

With this in mind, the Teacher begins with his oft-repeated lament, "I hated all the things I had toiled for," as he assessed the question of successors. He could only pronounce this state of affairs as meaningless (v. 19). If one's life work falls into the hands of a wise man, then well and good; but if a fool is the inheritor of a great man's work, then all the toil is of little use.

The Teacher adds further that "I turned about to cause my heart to despair" (v. 20, literal Hebrew; see also 7:25 concerning "I turned"). In other words, as he thinks of the consequences of to whom he would leave his inheritance, his heart is in a state of turmoil; and he is in despair. To make the point even sharper, he adds that he had not entered superficially into all his pursuits (v. 21). He labored with all his energies, as we saw already, using all his wisdom, knowledge, and skill. Will all this effort be taken for granted? Will posterity appreciate all the energy expended on building an empire by previous generations? Or will ungrateful children repudiate the values by which a previous generation provided a legacy? Will ease and comfort be taken for granted for which earlier generations struggled to provide? These are the kinds of questions that raced through the Teacher's mind and heart only to find these thoughts painful: "This too is meaningless and a great misfortune" or evil (v. 21).

Therefore, as the Teacher looked to the future, as he labored with the things under the sun, he did not have too much hope. It is natural for a person to always think of what is ahead and to plan accordingly. But the Teacher stated the issue honestly, "What does a man get for all the toil and anxious striving" (v. 22) if in the end no one can quite carry on the work and interests as he did? He says his task is painful and full of grief; and at night when man's heart reflects on the daily work, he has no rest or peace of mind at all (v. 23). Perhaps it might sound pessimistic, but actually the Teacher was only being realistic and truthful. In view of man's threescore and ten years and the toil with which he is engaged here on earth for his successors, the wise man was generally right with his concerns. Insofar as this world is concerned, both believer and unbeliever participate alike "under the sun"; and regardless of who the person is, he has to acknowledge the Teacher's conclusions so as to avoid life's pitfalls and try to enter into what can be enjoyed.

One observation must be made in all this discussion as we saw in the Introduction and which the Teacher will continually emphasize in his future discourses. As long as we keep God in the center of all of life's labors, we do not need to think only in terms of *this* life. The believer receives good advice from all this wisdom in what to expect from some pursuits and problems of this life; but having trusted in Christ, he also labors for higher values. Except for life's circumstances where there can be keen disappointment, the believer not only keeps one eye on how to live in this world, but he keeps his other eye on what comes after this life and which is no disappointment.

F. Yet There Is a Way to Enjoy Life (2:24–26)

The Teacher has shared with us his feelings and experiences as he searched for meaning in interests and work with all his energies. At successive phases in his life, he had his "kicks" in which he put his whole soul. He describes his disillusionment as in succession he abandoned one project and interest after another, pronouncing each one in turn as meaninglessness if this is all he lived for. It also was a pain to the Teacher to know that after working all his life in his many areas, he would have to give up everything, and in this respect he was no different than a fool. It was also meaningless and evil to know that his many productions would fall into the hands of those who did not know how to handle the inheritance and would even despise it.

In the face of such unhappy circumstances, is there anything in which a person could rejoice? The Teacher hastens to assure us that apart from the absolute sense, life can be enjoyed on the practical level and that this is even a gift of God, provided one keeps everything in balance. And so there is "nothing better than to eat and drink" (v. 24). There are differences as to how to translate the phrase "a man can do nothing better." Some want to put it into a negative frame, "It is not a good thing in man that he is able to eat and drink." (See Leupold, *Exposition of Ecclesiastes*, p. 75 and A. Cohen, ed., "Ecclesiastes" in *The Five Megillot*, p. 122, who notes what Rashi understood of this passage.) But it is unwarranted to impose the concept of man's sinfulness *here* as a contrast to the good things that come from the Lord. While the Teacher recognizes the sinfulness of man when he lives merely for the things of this life, yet he also insists that God is interested in man and wishes to provide him with the simple joys of life. It is from the hand of God that the basic things of life can be good and sweet.

Therefore, man can cause his soul to see good in his labor, provided that no one interest becomes an obsession or he tries to get more out of the things of this life than they can provide. So our eating and enjoyment cannot be without Him (v. 25). The Hebrew behind "Him" is actually "me," but the phrase "without Him" is supported by a number of versions as the most likely rendering. The translation provided by Robert Gordis, (p. 152), gives an interesting yet sobering touch concerning eating and having enjoyment: It is "except it be by His will."

The last verse in the conclusion might suggest that God is playing favorites: The man who pleases Him is blessed, and the sinner (see 8:12; 9:2; regarded also as a fool) can store up his money but must give it up in the long run to the one who pleases God (v. 26). As to why he is a sinner, we have to keep in mind the various areas of life already mentioned (1:12–2:11) in which a person can be involved and live only for those areas. Everyone can enjoy life, but we also have to remember the blessings of keeping proper perspectives in life.

The gifts God provides are often, the Teacher notes, based on a person's attitude. The one who is described as good in His sight is not perfect and without sin; but the one who has the right attitude and balance concerning the things of this life does have the promise from God of wisdom, knowledge, and happiness.

We have come to a sound conclusion after a wearying search. While there are many pitfalls and meaninglessnesses, yet there is a distinction between the one who pleases God and the sinner. The believer can have his gifts from God. But the people who live in sin and give their whole lives to amass fortunes, enjoy pleasures to the hilt, or pursue knowledge and education will live to realize that all they have achieved will go to the righteous ones. It becomes a bitter irony when God disposes all that has been gathered as He sees fit, and the experiences of sinners is meaninglessness and chasing after wind.

For Further Study

1. List and discuss several main considerations that guard the proper search for wisdom and knowledge.

2. Do you think society in general and the American taxpayer in particular would be better off with fewer professional scholars and professors in our state universities? Why or why not?

3. In Platonic thought there is an understanding, "To *know* the good means that one will *do* the good." What is your reaction to this assertion? Does the Teacher help us in answering this statement? If so, how?

4. List and discuss the four ways by which we can have pleasure to the fullest.

5. Were you ever involved in any of the pursuits of pleasure indicated by the Teacher? Can you put your finger on why it was so attractive?

6. What advice can you give young people growing up in Christian homes about avoiding the extremes of any of the pleasures the Teacher indicated?

7. Look up in a Bible dictionary the subject of water supply for ancient Jerusalem.

8. Would you say that American society is completely materialistic? If so, which area(s) of "things" would you advocate we use less of?

9. How do you react to the Teacher's descriptions of the toil of this life and what happens as we come to the end of life?

10. While we will discuss this issue later in this book, do you feel at this point a certain amount of uneasiness about the Teacher's advice that we can enjoy the things of this world? Why or why not?

Chapter 3

The Reality in Life's Pursuits
(Ecclesiastes 3:1–6:12)

We learned at the close of the last section, after a long struggle on the part of the Teacher, that God wants to provide us with the joys of life but in the proper context. We will discuss in this chapter the many features of experiences in life's pursuits. The Teacher lived a full life, and now he wants to share these with us—his insights, his good advice, and his frustrations.

A. The Use of Time Is God-Ordained (3:1–15)

In the Teacher's exposure to reality, he had to admit that often we are engaged in a work not of our own making; that is, while we are involved in activities of our own choice, we also are aware that we are somehow part of a plan that is greater than we are. We sense that after being engaged for many years in the affairs of this life and that no matter how intense may be our interest in any activity, we have to ask ourselves, "How free was I in the choice of such an activity?"

The Teacher lists a catalog of activities in fourteen pairs of opposites (v. 2–8) in the affairs of man when there is a specific season and time for them to occur (v. 1). Perhaps the list sounds discouraging when we realize that we are not the masters of our lives but that we seem to be controlled by the relentless round of seasons and the tide of events. We move from one activity to another, first one event and then its opposite. How are we to explain or understand this seeming senseless round of repetition?

A number of interpretations have been provided: 1) man has to do everything in its specific time, that is, be a Stoic and live according to the cycles of nature; 2) man finds life sheer monotony and all he does is repetitious; and 3) all man's involvement is useless because the Lord has predetermined everything in the round of life. (See Gordis who notes various interpretations, p. 228.) No doubt if we take any verse in verses 2–8 by itself, we can see how any of these interpretations might fit.

But the Teacher gives us some clue to his conclusions in verses 9–15. While he says that all human activities have their proper time, he goes beyond a superficial observation. Actually, he has two conclusions: 1) if the times and seasons are in the hands of God, then there is a sovereign action of God that transcends anything a man can do (v. 9); and 2) everything that will happen, even calamities, are part of God's plan (v. 11a). In 3:11b there is a disconcerting note. While man can understand something about eternity, yet it is a frustrating situation when he remains ignorant of a large part of what God has determined as good. If a person can realize that God is sovereign in His world, then there is a possibility for the believer to learn how to trust implicitly in the Lord. Hopefully, the unbeliever can also come to realize that it is best to know that God needs to be kept in the center of all thinking and activity and that man is not master of his own fate. Perhaps in the latter instance, the unbeliever could even entrust his soul to the Lord's keeping.

1. *For those times of life* (3:1–8)

The Teacher begins with the statement, "There is a time for everything, and a season for every activity under heaven" (v. 1). The Hebrew word for time (*'et*) refers to the proper, suitable time (BDB, p. 773) and the reference to season (*zeman*) is the emphasis on a specific time or particular season. Truly times and seasons are in God's hands to do and to dispose. The activities, or delights, man undertakes are within the limits He determines.

In the following verses (2–8), the word "time" is used twenty-eight times. The seven verses are so arranged that each verse has four parts where time is used. One is struck by the use of seven and its multiples; but numerics is a widely-used literary device. For example, in Genesis 12:2 and 3, seven promises are given to Abraham; Amos 1 and 2 mention seven nations; and Matthew 1 uses a multiple of seven, three groups of fourteen generations of the history of Israel (v. 17). No doubt this device was an aid to teach and to remember. At any rate, the Teacher describes many aspects of a person's life—his birth and end and all his hopes and sorrows in between.

Every person has his moment in time when he is born and dies (v. 1). Can any person ever say that "I wish I had been born at one point of time"? Perhaps parents may plan for the birth of their off-spring, but the children really have nothing to say about that. Neither do we predict our death date. The writer to the Hebrews says that we are destined for the particular time when we shall die, and we can neither hasten it nor prolong it (Heb. 9:27). To hasten one's death by suicide is actually homicide (Exod. 20:13). The point is that we have no control over these events; they are fixed times. In no way is the Teacher pessimistic; these are the facts of this world's existence.

Neither does the Teacher express his views on afterlife here. He is not going into a discussion on the intermediate state and the Resurrection because these topics are not within the scope of the book. He is concerned with what happens in this life, and believers should pay attention to life now as well as to what happens in the world to come. But there can be a testimony to unbelievers through the dying grace of godly people that God Himself has prepared for his children in the world to come. However, we must not read more into the book than what the Teacher purposed to do.

The wise man continues this discussion of time concerning plant life (v. 2b). There are times when plants, vines, and trees are planted because there is an ordained order of the planting season. Wheat is not planted in the dead of winter; there are specified times when fruit trees are planted. The farmer cannot go against an ordained time when planting must take place; and the Teacher was aware of this fact because he had parks, fruit trees, and all kinds of growing things in his vineyards, gardens, and orchards (2:5–6). Similarly, there are times when fruit trees must be uprooted because they no longer bear fruit; there are times vineyards have to be rooted up when they have fallen prey to disease. Growing things are not exempt from nonproductivity and death any more than human beings. There is a time when plants and trees die, as painful as it is to see.

The time to kill sounds harsh to Christians who abhor the thought (v. 3a). Even unbelievers are revulsed by the news media, which bring to the television screen the horrors of war, its attendant death scenes, and the suffering of the living. Again the Teacher does not sanction such activities but merely recognizes that in a world of unre-generate men there will be individuals and nations who will suffer the judgment of God when He decrees their death and destruction. World

War II is a good example of God's providential rule among nations to curb evil (Dan. 4:17). The same is true for believers when they persist in their wrongdoing; many Christians have been taken home before their time so that God's work should not be affected (1 Cor. 11:29–32).

God does give healing as well, and after great conflicts there comes the time of peace and a time to forget the horrors of war and death. Man rebuilds what was torn down, even as it happened after World War II. This is true also for God's people when they have been disciplined, "He has torn us to pieces but he will heal us; he has injured us but he will bind up our wounds" (Hos. 6:1). Precious indeed are those times when the sinner returns home (Luke 15:20) or when a nation turns to the Lord (Judg. 2:18).

The Teacher continues his parallelism in verse 3b. In time of war there is destruction of property along with the loss of life. When the Babylonians came under Nebuchadnezzar, they destroyed the wall and then broke into the Temple area and destroyed Solomon's Temple (2 Kings 25). In modern warfare the loss in property and material possessions is beyond measure. World War II is an eloquent testimony to this statement when the providential rule of God permitted this loss in order to bring people to Himself. Yet there is also the time to build up. After the seventy years were accomplished for Judah in exile, the promise of Jeremiah the prophet was fulfilled when God's people were permitted to return and build again the Temple and the walls around the city (Jer. 24:6, 7). Perhaps one might also see that rebuilding is not just in material means alone. "To build up" also can have a spiritual connotation because Jeremiah prophesied that besides the restoration of the land of Judah, God promised to the exiles who returned a new heart to know Him.

There are those times when we weep (v. 4) and when we mourn as a result of the events of verses 2 and 3. Life has its problems and its heartrending experiences when tears flow down the cheeks. The griefs associated with death, illness, and losses are a part of life; and often it is in the valley of emotions that we learn our most precious experiences of what it means to trust. God can in many ways comfort those who mourn (Matt. 5:4) and demonstrate to us that He really does care. If the person is not a believer, it may be in these times of lamentation that he or she finds the Lord.

But we can also praise the Lord that weeping and mourning do not last forever. There will be times to laugh and dance. Achievements, weddings, births of children are all occasions that are the joys of life. God gives us these times of refreshing. The reference to "dancing" is either to the group dancing, which is so much a part of the land of Israel (similar to square dancing in the United States), or to the kind of dancing in which David was engaged when the ark was brought into the area where the first temple was to stand. That occasion was a time to laugh and rejoice because of God's goodness.

What does it mean to scatter and gather stones (v. 5)? Some interpret this verse in connection with stone work and wish to spiritualize the passage to describe the corruption of the church (Leupold, p. 87). What needs to be remembered is that verses 2–8 follow the pattern of Hebrew poetry, and each verse exhibits synonymous parallelism. This means that the second line of a verse can throw light on what is meant in the first line.

Verse 5b is a description of those times when embracing and love-making are in order, but there are occasions when this display of affection is not appropriate. Therefore, this line could clarify the first one. The Midrash, or Jewish commentary, on Kohelet says of this verse, "A time to cast stones—when your wife is clean, and time to gather stones in—when your wife is unclean (her period)," a reference to relations of the husband and wife (see Gordis, p. 230). Or it could picture the more simple sense of comparison. As there is a time to embrace a wife or abstain, so there is a time to gather up precious stones for building purposes and to discard useless stones. The same objects or persons can be treated differently on various occasions.

There are times when we search for lost possessions and keep what is appropriate (v. 6). On the other hand, when we cannot find what was lost, we give up the search because the time expended is not commensurate with the value of the lost article. There are times when we throw away what is no longer valuable or useful. The Teacher's advice is most apropos as we contemplate what we have stored away in our attics and closets. In fact, much of what we have has long outlasted its usefulness and should therefore be tossed out. Our problem too often is that we cling too much to things; then after we go, we do not take them with us but rather leave them to others to clean up!

There is a time to tear apart and a time to mend (v. 7). "Tearing" or "rending" may well refer to the rending of garments in the time of mourning. In the Middle East this was a prevalent custom (Gen. 37:29;

2 Sam. 13:31); it continued through the centuries and can still be seen today among many peoples. Conversely, mending describes the sewing of the tear after the period of mourning is over. The parallelism is continued in the second line; in the period of mourning, silence is observed (Lev. 10:3; Job 2:13). People in mourning resumed their normal speech only after the mourning period was over.

We now come to the end of the many activities that are a part of life, and the Teacher can hardly finish without mentioning love and hate, which are strong emotional expressions (v. 8). Made in the image of God, a person does have the capacity to love to a certain degree. A man and wife marry because of love, establish a home, raise a family; and everyone in the family shows affection and love for one another. If one of the children is ill, father and mother care for their offspring because of their love that commits them. Many are the situations where a spouse falls ill and the partner lovingly tends his or her beloved. But love can turn to hatred; and where once a person has loved dearly, especially a wife or husband, a fierce hatred can be the result. One can hate with all the soul, particularly when infidelity is the case. Both on a personal level as well as national, love and good will can turn to hatred with individuals fighting and nations going to war.

2. *Considerations of time and eternity* (3:9-15)

The Teacher now raises the same question found in 1:3: What is the profit or advantage (*yitron*, 1:10) of all these experiences within time? Is he being negative? Perhaps! On the other hand, there is also the recognition that man is part of the round of changes within time and circumstances over which he really has no control. The point then suggests that it is useless for a person to put forth any effort to avert the times and the circumstances. One needs to gracefully accept the times that God has ordained.

The Teacher hastens to add that he sees, or understands, the burden with which men occupy themselves. We agree that he has researched well all the occupations that bring on great trouble and cost so much effort. The Hebrew word for "burden" is the same as in 1:13 where it is rendered "heavy burden" and in 2:26 where it has the idea of a task or form of business. Here it is merely the continual burden with which men are engaged during a lifetime; but rather than becoming morose, the Teacher immediately propels us to another consideration in verse 11. The times ordained by God in which men work are not to be seen as something settled in concrete. Rather, we see an unfolding pattern where life refuses to stay still for even one moment. In fact, God has indeed made everything beautiful! The Teacher has come to realize that God is working in a dynamic way as He unfolds His will, a masterpiece of the one Creator. Therefore, the events of 3:2–8 are to be seen as a part of the whole plan of God. Taken in isolated pieces, each of the "times" appears to be ugly with no meaning; but when it is seen as God sees it, there is a beautiful pattern to the plan.

In struggling with the events of time, the Teacher now reveals an amazing fact: He discovers that he does have a sense of eternity (v. 11). As he has observed the present with its many different kinds of "times," he realizes that this has been built on a long series of events in the past. But as the experiences of the present continue, there is a pathway to the future. In a rare glimpse, he reveals that God has given him the perception of eternity; and this, more than any other reason, reveals that man is at the pinnacle of God's creation.

While occasionally he sees a glimpse of God's high and holy purposes in the vertical plane, he does not see all of what God is doing from his horizontal view. Man as a mortal creature does not see as God sees, the whole and the entire, from the beginning even to the end.

This incomprehensibility of life can be quite unsettling. The secularist can struggle as well as the believer. Certainly all people try to make the best of what life has to offer in spite of the difficulty of understanding it. Therefore, the Teacher encourages all people to be happy and do good (literally, "to get good") as long as they live (3:12). The best that the secularist can do in view of his struggle with life is to try and enjoy himself in his search for good. The believer, however, can trust God; while he too may struggle with life, he realizes that God is merciful and never takes him beyond what he can bear. For sure, life can be enjoyed; and wherever one finds good, he is able to eat and drink and even see satisfaction in all his toil. It is all a gift from God (3:13). This search for pleasure and the "getting of good" has already been discussed, but one does not make this the sole object of existence that can become only meaningless. Taken in moderation, God can send joy to a person's heart even though he might find life extremely difficult.

The Teacher now concludes his discussion regarding the use of time as God has ordained (3:14–15). Based on the facts of his experience, the events of the round of life are designed to teach men to revere, or

stand in awe of Him. (See also 5:7; 7:18; 8:12–13; this truth is promi-
nently emphasized.) To revere God is the beginning of wisdom and
calls for a trust in Him and His purposes.

Man cannot alter the circumstances through which he passes. Whatever is has already been and what will be has been before, an observation already made (1:9). The laws of God do not change; the world is
created in accordance with natural and moral laws, and these continue
in their appointed times. But this design of life is such that man is
encouraged to look beyond himself to the higher Power, recognize His
purposes, and trust Him.

We almost lose the thought, therefore, when we come to "God will
call the past to account" (3:15c). The passage is rendered differently by
various versions and commentators: "God seeks what has passed by"
(NASV); "driven away" (ARV margin); "God seeks the persecuted"
(Hengstenberg, Septuagint, and other Greek translations); "the one
pursued or persecuted" (Luther). Perhaps the best that can be said is
that there is certainly a round of life in accordance with His laws that
have existed in the past and will continue to exist in the future as long
as the present earth remains. Therefore, at any time in the future, God
can reach into the past and bring forth what is necessary for the future,
for the ongoing of His plan, or to confront man in judgment for deeds
long forgotten in the past. From God's point of view, He is the One
who can establish the link between the past and the future.

We therefore conclude this emphasis on the use of time and realize
that one needs to harmonize with the times and seasons ordained of
God. As mortal creatures we do not see the whole picture as God sees
it; at times we may see some aspects of God's works, but in most
instances we do not. In the round of life we learn to revere God, stand
in awe before Him, and try to make the best of life as it comes to us.
The believer has to recognize and trust God in the midst of life's
circumstances. After all, if God can plan the vast universe, then certainly He at the same time does not forget man.

B. Human Injustice, a Matter of Life and Death, and Perversity (3:16–4:3)

We have just considered how God rules His world in accordance
with set times and seasons, yet man often does not acknowledge God's
sovereignty. While God is faithful to believers and unbelievers, some
men can run the affairs of this world as if there were no God. In the end

it will seem, however, that all men are but puny at best if they think they are greater than God.

1. *How the wicked seem almighty* (3:16–17)

The Teacher had lived long enough to observe the unfortunate experience that in the place of judgment, that is, where an objective judgment should be made with fairness to all concerned, wickedness prevails (3:16a). The word for wickedness pictures a bent justice and human rights that have been perverted. To emphasize the point, the observation also underscores the fact that in the place of justice where a subjective righteousness and righteous action should be present on the part of the judge or ruler, only wickedness prevails (3:16b). This is not the first time that the Teacher dwells on this issue; it occurs at intervals in passages yet to come. Too often judges and rulers are bribed and justice is corrupted.

The Teacher reacts and expects God to take the situation in hand and judge the wicked, either immediately or at some time in the future, and rightly so (v. 17). Obviously, however, people usually want immediate action and are impatient with the delay. Nevertheless, God will care for the innocent and judge the guilty. The sentence includes the word "there," for "there will be a time for every activity." In Hebrew this word is last in the sentence; and Leupold suggests that the Teacher, while speaking, could have pointed toward heaven where God is and stated emphatically that He will judge every inequity even though man might feel that He had overlooked it (p. 95). The seeming almighty wicked will be brought low.

2. *A matter of life and death* (3:18–21)

The theme of judgment in 3:16–17 is carried forward by the Teacher to demonstrate that wicked man is not as high and mighty as he thinks he is (v. 18). He is not judged immediately for his wrong choices because God can delay His interference into the affairs of man in order to let him make decisions in his own way. God's intention is to test man, that is, to sift man so that what is in his heart can become evident. Man needs the experiences of life in order to reveal what is in his heart, either for good or evil, depending on the moral choices he makes. In the time within the crucible of experience men can see for themselves that if they make a practice of perverting justice and righteousness, they are like the animals. The point can well be taken that if the wicked ignore the fact that God will interpose His judgment at some time in the future and lose sight of God, then they are no different than the animal. The psalmist also reminds us that the Lord looks down from heaven to see if there are men who understand, who seek God (Ps. 14:2). Wicked man struts on earth's scene, but he is puny at best.

We come to what some feel to be the most puzzling statements in Ecclesiastes (vv. 19–21). Taken out of context they can be misused by many cultists, as indicated in the Introduction, but we cannot lose sight of the overall view of the Teacher in his observations.

This matter of comparing wicked man and the animals leads the Teacher to make some further comparisons. Perhaps he is trying to underscore the point of how a man can think of himself as being beyond question for his actions in taking advantage of the weak and the poor. If man will not listen to the fact that God will bring all things into judgment, then he ought to at least think in terms of the day of his death. This point is mentioned in later Jewish thought; if a person does not repent, then as a last appeal he is advised to think of the day of his death!

In a wider sense, however, why are men and animals compared in death? Perhaps there is the tendency to become pessimistic because, from this world's view, as we come to the end of life, whether man or animal, all do die. Certainly it does appear that there is a vast qualitative difference between man and the animal. Yet because man is a mortal creature, there is also a tremendous similarity between himself and the animal. One breath (*ruaḥ* or spirit) is in both of them. We are reminded of that which perished in the flood, man and beast, "Everything . . . that had the breath of life in its nostrils" (Gen. 7:22). The "everything" includes man and animal, all living creatures; they have the *ruaḥ* (spirit) for in the Genesis passage all living creatures, man and animal, have literally "the breath of the spirit of life." But breath and spirit are interchanged in 3:19, using this designation as a characteristic that both man and animal possess to demonstrate the similarity of the two.

From the merely human point of view, therefore, man dies—even as animals die—when he comes to the end of his life. The point is carried forward in verse 20. The bodies of both man and animal are made of the chemicals of the earth; when the end of life comes, both man and animals die, and the bodies of each disintegrate back into the dust of the earth (Gen. 3:19; Ps. 104:29).

The Teacher now raises a question as to what happens after death with a: "Who knows?" (v. 21). Does the breath (Hebrew, spirit) ascend upward while that of the breath (again, spirit) of the animal descend downward? In verse 20 he made a comparison between man and animals, that both eventually die; now he goes beyond death to see the decided difference between the two.

Is he raising a question concerning existence after death as if he has no idea? That depends on how we translate the verse: 1) who knows *whether* (or if) the spirit of man . . . *whether* (or if) the spirit of the beast . . .; or 2) that *the* spirit of man . . . that *the* spirit of the beast. . . . In the first possibility, an interrogative qualifies spirit of man and beast as if there was a question concerning what happens to man and beast after death. In the second suggestion a definite article stands in front of the spirit of man and the spirit of the beast, which means that the Teacher had a very definite idea of the difference of the fate for man and beast because he is not raising questions about "whether." This writer opts for the second suggestion because it is more in line with the world view of the Teacher; for example, the wicked will meet God in final judgment (3:17); and we are warned as to how we are to live in this world because there will be a judgment in the end when we shall have to give an account of every deed (12:14). What is the point of the warning if man merely dies as the animals and that is all there is to it? No, the Teacher had a concept of immortality that reflected what many believed in the community of Israel. The Psalm of the sons of Korah, in a statement of faith, indicated that "God will redeem my soul from the grave (Sheol); he will surely take me to himself" (Ps. 49:15). People in the Old Testament did have a word from God that man is indeed different from the animal.

We now can understand better the question raised by the Teacher, "Who knows?" He had in mind a kind of warning to those who would be flippant and not believe that man does have a future after this life. If that is so, then one's moral choices do not matter and man can live as he pleases. The appeal then is directed as follows: "Who among you will only listen and realize that man is different from the animal and that he has to give an account of himself when life comes to an end?"

Are we morbid talking about death and all this discussion concerning man and animals and what happens after death? Our approach in the modern sense to the concern of death is to push the prospect out of mind or try to shield ourselves from the harsh reality of death. Our funeral parlors smell nice, and the funeral cosmetics for the dead are "beautiful." The aged are in senior citizens' homes, and rest homes are in appropriate aesthetic surroundings. But not so in the ancient world. Death was not covered up, and the aged were in full view of everyone in their families. Therefore, the Teacher speaks from a position of reality and sets before us the prospect that death is very much a part of life. We cannot avoid it.

Even though we have to face death, we are not to become pessimistic. For both believer and unbeliever, as long as there is the opportunity and the capacity, he or she can be happy in all of life's work (3:22). God desires that man should be involved in his portion even though from earth's viewpoint he does not see too clearly what will happen to him after this life. The premium is on a job that is well done; and, in fact, work is an involvement that carries with it a blessing from God. There is much that each one can enjoy in the pursuits of life in this world, knowing that God will in the end evaluate our lives.

3. *Perversity and hard questions* (4:1–3)

The Teacher now comes back to the theme that he began in 3:16: the acts of oppression that are committed under the sun. Once again he saw and understood an extremely painful situation. The experience was a curse in the day in which he lived as it is a real curse today as well. All too often a few seem to have the power to control the masses and cause untold suffering and misery. Twice the phrase is repeated that the oppressed have no one to comfort them and the world was nothing more than a veil of tears.

In no way is the Teacher fatalistic. It is a hard fact that we live in a world where oppression is on every hand, but there are those occasions when the burdens of the oppressed are lifted as God in His providential rule can and does intervene among the nations to control evil and do away with wicked rulers who abuse the masses. When new rulers come on the scene, however, they often are no better than the previous ones; and once again people suffer with tears running down their faces.

These observations were expressed by others in many circumstances. David at one time looked for sympathy from his oppressors, but there was none (Ps. 69:20). Jerusalem had no one to comfort her after she had been sacked and destroyed (Lam. 1:2). James calls it a great virtue to visit and comfort those who are in distress and really need a helpful fellowship (James 1:27).

The Teacher's final comment on these sets of circumstances startles us because of what seems a sad conclusion, but again he is not cynical or fatalistic. He claims those who have died appear to be better off than those who suffer the untold agony of oppression with no comfort and no relief in sight. Elijah cried to the Lord to be taken home (1 Kings 19:4). The black people for decades, in the midst of oppression, sang their songs and spirituals which always have had the theme of the hope that they be removed from this earth's scene: "Swing low, sweet chariot, comin' for to carry me home"; and "Deep River . . . my home is over Jordan." Many other spirituals likewise have their emphasis on the time of release from the burdens, tears, and oppressions of this life.

The Teacher adds that it would be even better if we never saw the light of day than to enter into all the evil activity we find in so many situations here in this life. Is he given to excessive gloom? Job expressed similar sentiments when he cried out that nonexistence is better than the suffering of his misery (Job 3:3–10). We certainly can see worldwide misery a lot more today than the ancients did: the suffering and death of Jewish people in the concentration camps of World War II, the slaughter of millions of peasants in the Russian Ukraine in the 1930s because they defied Stalin, the thousands of Japanese who suffered horribly from the radiation after the atom bombs were dropped on Hiroshima and Nagasaki. No wonder people wish they had never been born! Nevertheless, the realities of life are in many ways the same in every generation, and the desire to escape from them is as real today as it was in the Teacher's day. As he contemplated the many experiences of tragedy, illness, and horrors, he was only being realistic, particularly concerning people who have no opportunity for the hope that characterizes the believer.

C. Competition and the Money-Maker (4:4–8)

Once again the Teacher meditates on certain activities taken to the extreme (v. 4). He saw people who worked hard with their skills. The word "skills" (see 2:21) has the idea that there are those who can achieve as they do a skillful piece of work. But for what purpose? Involvement with business too often is more than just friendly rivalry with competitors. It is a human trait to achieve; but in the "law of the jungle" in the business world, a person can be extremely jealous of his neighbor's accomplishments. All of us at times want to be at our best so that others can admire us, but it is human to strive to reach the top because we envy others who have become successful. The Teacher certainly knew something about this trait in the areas of which he spoke before concerning pleasure and material achievements. If the motive for success is tainted, then how can achievement actually satisfy? The Teacher is correct, then, in assessing such activity as meaningless and chasing after the wind.

If success can be gained by trying to get the best of a fellow human being, then the extreme opposite is the fool, the idle person, as he folds his hands and ruins himself by doing nothing (v. 5; Prov. 6:10). Such a person only wastes his possessions, thereby losing his grasp of the world's reality, the care for his own person, and eventually even his own self-respect.

The Teacher has an answer, based on his own experience with life, to both attitudes of overwork to build his empire at the expense of others or just simply doing nothing (v. 6). His advice is to have one hand full with tranquility or rest, literally a restfulness of mind, rather than two handfuls of toil. Competition because of envy does not give a person rest at all while trying to double the amount one has. In addition, the one handful is far better than the fool with his nothingness and emptiness. Once again the Teacher strives for a moderation in life that avoids the deadly extremes.

But if envy can be soul-consuming, the Teacher also reminds us that a man who lives only for the purpose of being a money-maker is nothing more than a downright hoarder (vv. 7–8). Here is a man all alone, with no dependents, working at full capacity; the description of him is disgusting. His eyes are never satisfied, and he has become a miser, never content with what he has and continually demanding more. Where will it all end? The Teacher seems to paraphrase the question for this person that he should be asking himself: "For whom am I toiling and why am I depriving myself of enjoyment?" Such a person is actually lonely; but many fit this description and are involved in this kind of activity. Can business and moneymaking fill the void? Once again this extreme brings on the Teacher's assessment, a word that he himself also learned through bitter experience. Moneymaking in itself is only meaningless and empty and certainly a miserable business. We must learn to avoid the extremes, or we will be frustrated and will not have the maximum benefits of life. Solomon's suggestion is a truth that can be taken to heart, "Better a little with righteousness than much gain with injustice" (Prov. 16:8). Paul's advice is also to the point, "Godliness with contentment is great gain" (1 Tim. 6:6).

D. Companionship and Fleeting Acclaim (4:9–16)

1. *The value of contentment* (4:9–12)

Having observed the lonely miser, the Teacher now turns naturally to discuss companionship and its benefits. Partners who work together in harmony can produce better results and reap more profits than when each of them works by himself (v. 9). If one should fall in his toil or in a literal fall, the other would stand by his side to help him (v. 10). Faithful friends who stand at our side are a precious gift in life. We are reminded that we must not stand alone and that we really need each other. The writer can only cry out in a pathetic tone for the one who stands by himself. When he falls, who will help him? Loneliness reaps a horrible price, and one of the greatest lessons of life is to realize that we are social creatures. We need companionship—as marriage partners, fellow workers in business, or school chums—to help each of us develop and mature our personalities. The single person follows a course contrary to what God designed us to be.

The benefits of companionship also are seen in reference to travelers who sleep together on a cold night, a situation that sounds strange to our western ears (v. 11). Winter nights can be cold in the land of Israel, and one's covering was extremely important to keep warm (Exod. 22:26–27; Isa. 28:20). Even better was the huddling together of two or more for warmth. The description could also refer to the way a family shared a bed to keep warm (Luke 11:7). But what happens to the lone individual who has no companions and who must suffer and be extremely uncomfortable when it is cold? His loneliness will only be accentuated.

Our society today is not unique with its record of mugging and assault. The Teacher also had in mind similar occasions in his day, particularly when traveling (v. 12). The loner had little protection when attacked by robbers. If, however, two were traveling together, or worked together, there was less likelihood of assault. When it did occur, two could better overcome their attackers.

To further press the point, three working together are even better than the two to ward off robbers. The Teacher seems to follow the pattern provided in Proverbs by using the technique of the numerical proverb: six things the Lord hates, yes, even seven (Prov. 6:16); three things that are too amazing for me, even four (Prov. 30:18). So the point of the cord of three strands not quickly broken emphasizes the formidable bond of three working together as companions who can withstand most assaults. This proverb and other descriptions in Jewish literature underscore the value of friends who cooperate in their work.

2. *How fleeting is man's acclaim* (4:13–16)

The Teacher turns his attention to still another series of events he has observed on the political scene. Rulers, after being entrenched in power for too long, are replaced by those who come out of poverty and anonymity. He is not speaking of his own situation; but rather, the Teacher from his own vantage point had opportunity to observe what had occurred to many kings and chiefs in a number of countries of his day. The incident to which he referred could have been well-known to people then but is not known to us from any historical records.

The description of a king who has grown old and out of touch with the needs of his people is all too familiar (v. 13). The ruler has forgotten his earlier circumstances from which he had come to take the leadership, and across the years he has insulated himself from the needs of his people. He has come to enjoy the benefits of rulership; he is taken up with those around him who cater to his every whim and pleasure. The Teacher's assessment is that such a person has grown old and become foolish, even senile, and can no longer adequately rule. No doubt the old ruler has allowed the government to become corrupt, and lesser officials are becoming rich as they oppress the poor. This situation has many modern counterparts.

Such a state of affairs can only breed discontent, and it will not be long before some enterprising young person will seize power to rectify deplorable political and economic affairs (v. 14). The Teacher's observation of this young person is that he is at least better than the old and foolish king. The young ruler is more in touch with the needs of the oppressed and downtrodden people and may even have firsthand knowledge of those who have been imprisoned for one offense or another. The new ruler could even have been imprisoned himself because of his rebellion against the corrupt rulership of the old king. Often in His providential rulership, God will permit the upstarts in a rebellion to seize power in order to correct the excesses of a regime that no longer cares for its subjects.

The word for youth is the Hebrew *yeled*, used many times to describe one who has not reached the years of puberty; but it can also be used of one older than a mere child. *Yeled* describes Joseph when he was seventeen (Gen. 37:30) and the friends of Rehoboam when the latter was over forty years old (1 Kings 12:8). The point perhaps is the sharp contrast between the young person and the old but foolish king.

Obviously, when a young person is able to overthrow a corrupt regime, he will have many followers who will want to benefit themselves where previously they had little or nothing. We can imagine that the young ruler will be idolized by the people who will acclaim their new champion.

The new and young king starts well (vv. 15, 16a). But what happens when a new generation comes on the scene (v. 16b)? As the new ruler in turn becomes old, he will go the way of the former king, no doubt not having learned from previous experiences. In turn the new ruler, as he tastes of the victories of his success, allows them to go to his head and becomes much like his predecessor. A new generation that follows will be displeased with him, and the process will repeat itself all over again. The tragedy, the Teacher observes, is that very few learn from their experiences; and to view this process in repetition is a meaninglessness and a chasing after the wind. The time of acclaim lasts only for a few fleeting years that pass all too quickly. "What fools we mortals be," is a modern description of these situations where rulers try to hold on to power and people want to change the government.

E. Interlude: Instructions for Effective Worship (5:1–7)

This writer feels that there is now an interlude among the many difficult realities in life that the Teacher discusses. Sometimes these breaks prevent what might become a too pessimistic assessment of life and allow for a balance so as to consider the vertical look in one's relationship with God. We are enabled thereby to realize the influence of the divine King who brings some sanity into the round of life which by itself can be dreary and cheerless. Worship is one of those positive experiences that give one the lift to face difficult realities.

(If the reader is following a Hebrew Bible, then he will note that 5:1 is actually 4:17 in Hebrew. This Hebrew division also is followed by the Greek Septuagint and the Latin Vulgate. The difference of one verse continues through this chapter to 6:1 where both the Hebrew and English versions coincide again.)

Out of his vast experience in relationship with the world and God, the Teacher now offers his advice on one's attitude and approach to the divine King. A person is encouraged to worship God and go to His house. The admonition to guard one's steps in the approach to God stresses the fact that respect and honor must be given to Him who alone is almighty and holy (v. 1a). The "house of God" is understood to be the temple at Jerusalem with which the Teacher was involved at its dedication. We see this term elsewhere in 1 Chronicles 9:11. The synagogues in the pre-exilic period had not yet become an institution, and neither were they designated as "houses of God" until a much later date in the second temple period (from about 300–200 B.C. onward).

In one's approach to God the wise advice is to draw near to the Ruler of the universe to listen (v. 1b), that is, to hear the Word of God that was supposed to be taught in His house. Obviously, when one listens with his heart, he will be more ready to obey. To know how to obey God will depend on how sharp an interest with which we listen. Such an attitude is more desirable than the fools who come with their sacrifice offerings. The reason they are fools is that they do not listen and therefore are ignorant. For this reason they do evil because sacrifice for them is mere ritual to get over with as soon as possible.

We found earlier in the wisdom literature that the more proper worship was to do what was right and just rather than offer a mere ritual sacrifice to the Lord (Prov. 21:3). Samuel had already stated this truth in his assessment of Saul's ministry (1 Sam. 15:22f.). In no way does this truth endorse the critical notion that the prophets and sages were encouraging moral behavior and the cessation of the sacrifices. The correct procedure in Old and New Testament worship is to offer sacrifices and gifts to God, along with the right heart attitude that listens to His instructions.

The Teacher also had his grievance with repetition of prayer for he considered it to be a rapid chatter of meaningless words and he warned the worshiper not to be quick or rash with his mouth (v. 2). The danger here is that one who is quick with his mouth usually does not have too much thought behind the words. In this respect, a number of Jewish commentators (i.e., Rashi, Halevi) have warned that glib words can lead a person to even criticize God for permitting evil in the world. Rash speech moves so easily from criticizing the little things of life to questioning the high and lofty purposes of God!

The second line of the verse repeats the warning of the first, that one must not be hasty in his heart. The wrong desires of the heart that find expression on the tongue must be curbed. The helpful instruction to counterbalance the wrong heart attitude and senseless chatter is a reminder that the worshiper stands before the high, lofty, and holy God. He is in heaven; that is, He is infinite in His greatness and majesty, and man should be humble before Him. It is best always to maintain a humble heart and to let words be few in God's presence. After all, He hears us and knows the intent behind the words. Jesus Himself warned against a lot of babbling (Matt. 6:7); and in the model for prayer He reminds us that as we pray to the "Father in heaven," we must appreciate the fact that we stand before a God of infinite greatness and wisdom. Why then do a lot of superficial talking in prayer when a few choice, wise words will accomplish even more good?

Dreams are very much a part of the human experience, particularly when a person is caught up with the many cares of his work and relationships with people (v. 3). He may be very worried about his work during the day; as a result, dreams can disturb him at night when he ought to sleep peacefully. This very ordinary experience becomes a helpful parallelism; as many cares lead to many disturbing dreams, so many words describe the speeches of a fool. When a person speaks too much with his many words in the presence of God, he only makes a fool of himself. Prayers can be prattling without any meaning. It is interesting to note that when Moses prayed on behalf of Miriam in her leprous condition, he merely said, "O God, please heal her!" (Num. 12:13). In Hebrew this prayer consists of a mere five monosyllables, and yet God heard him to answer in a mighty way.

The Teacher now takes up the issue of vows made to God (vv. 4–7). If there was anything that disgruntled him, it was the making of vows that were not kept. In a sense this is also one form of talking too much.

The instructions concerning vows were given by Moses in Deuteronomy 23:21–23. When they are made to God, there should be no delay in paying them; God has a right to require payment in full, and to not pay is considered sin before God. It is better not to vow, in which case the person will not be held guilty. The point is that a person's words should mean something, particularly when he has made a promise to the Lord. Once again, it is a question of how fools talk too much and thereby make rash promises before God. When it comes time to pay up on the promise and the temple official comes to collect, only a fool would dare say that his vow was a mistake. Such a person stands in danger of losing everything in the long run, even as Ananias and Sapphira learned in their bitter experience (Acts 5:1–11). Their promise to give their all was in a sense a vow; but by withholding part of it, they not only reneged on the promise but also lied! Therefore, the Teacher warns, stand in awe before God; and avoid many meaningless words that can lead only to foolishness and downright sin (v. 7).

The Teacher shows a depth of appreciation of God's presence and has a good grasp on correct relationships that avoid mere formal approach to the divine King. This belies the concept that he was a hopeless cynic. Indeed, he was not!

F. The Vice of Bureaucracy (5:8–9)

The discussion shifts back again from worship to the horizontal view of life's realities to consider how officials deal corruptly in their relations with the public. This plague is ever present, and as soon as one set of corrupt officials are thrown out, another group comes on the scene.

By no means is the Teacher calloused when he tells us we should not be surprised when the poor are oppressed and their justice and rights are taken away (v. 8). He was relating the sad but true assessment of a bureaucracy's corruption. The reference to districts indicates areas far removed from the center of authority. Therefore, oppression often started on the lowest levels where lowly officials took more from the people than what was normally to come from them. In this respect they were watched by the next higher officials who in turn took their share of the spoils. Above all of them were the officers of the state who also had to be enriched. Those who suffered the worst were the poor at the low levels as they had to support the entire corrupt system while all the officials fattened their bank accounts. As it was in the ancient world of the Teacher, so it is true in succeeding centuries. We see the system in the first century as each level of tax collectors gouged the poor in order to support the Roman government with all of its corruption in the land of Israel. How this description is true even today!

What has value in an agricultural economy is the profit that comes from the land (v. 9). The king and the court that served him were supported by the fields. As soon as unused land was cultivated, every official up and down the line insisted on his share of what could be obtained from it. Some interpreters suggest that the king devoted himself to agriculture as he cultivated his field, but such an interpretation of verse 9 does not follow from what is indicated in the context of the preceding verse. Once again the Teacher spells out the situations as they are, and his purpose is not to deal with revolution to correct the deplorable situation. Even if a revolt took place, in the long run we would only see a return to an original corruption. The Teacher knew what is in the heart of man when, given half a chance, he reverts to corruption and oppression when he is in power. Occasionally, when a king or ruler curbs corruption and gives the working man his rights, then that regime is blessed indeed of God.

G. The Grasp for Money (5:10–6:6)

Now that the Teacher has introduced the deplorable evils of an economic system where officials grab for more and more, he takes up the subject of money and the dangers it can pose when it is in the wrong hands.

1. Money in itself is never able to satisfy (5:10–12)

Paul's warnings in the New Testament, "For the love of money is a root of all kinds of evil" and that "some people, eager for money, have wandered from the faith and pierced themselves with many griefs" (1 Tim. 6:10), have a precedent in what the Teacher cautioned. If a person lives only for money, he will never have enough because the love for money has within it the desire and itch for more (v. 10a). Rabbinic wisdom also reminds us, "Who is rich? He who rejoices in his portion" (Sayings of the Fathers 4:1). In the parallel expression (v. 10b), the Teacher continues the idea; he who loves his wealth or abundance acquired through crafty bargaining in the noisy marketplace will never be satisfied with what he obtains. This wise man put his finger on the psychological makeup of the money-grabbing person who is never content and lacks fulfillment. Such is the picture of a money-hungry, corrupt official as well as the rich man who never has enough. The end result of a life where money is the only object is truly an emptiness and meaninglessness, a conclusion the Teacher already had determined (2:11).

Another picture of the lack of satisfaction in what money itself can supply is the observation that as goods increase (literally, "when that which is good increases"), the man who grows wealthier will find he has to support a more complex establishment (v. 11). His servants and "friends" multiply ever more. But the Teacher asks a telling question: What benefit (advantage, 2:22) is it to the owner of all this wealth?

Does he really enjoy it? All he can do is feast his eyes on the sight of his riches. He cannot really enjoy them because they are all consumed by his numerous staff who must manage them.

Still another description is the contrast between the ordinary working man and the rich man. The abundance or satiety of the wealthy person seems to refer to the largest amount a person could ever want. The rich man has many possessions at his disposal, but all of these things do not permit him to sleep (v. 12). He is filled with projects, cares, and anxieties that he takes with him to bed; and the mind simply cannot rest. On the other hand, the laborer, even though he works hard and eats his full (or he may not even have enough to eat), enjoys sweet sleep. He simply is not bothered by a multitude of difficult problems and generally can enjoy a refreshing, sound rest.

2. *Money is easily lost* (5:13–14)

The Teacher is pained to the inner core when he has to make the observation concerning how wealth can be lost. He says that it is a grievous evil, literally a sick evil.

He refers to a man who has amassed a fortune, and he merely hoards it (v. 13). Instead of using what he has made for his own comfort or for that of his family, he clasps it to his bosom and eventually suffers because of it. He might become sick with worry over his money, whether he will lose it or it will be taken from him. People can even curse the one who withholds that which can be of help to those who are less fortunate (Prov. 11:26).

Worse tragedies are those experiences whereby wealth is lost through bad business deals or business failure. While such cases do not occur every day, the possession of wealth always carries with it the uncertainty of continuous possession. Others will try to get their hands on it. The Teacher illustrated this by telling how a man labored with all his might to amass his fortune and then lost it altogether (v. 14). He thought perhaps he could pass it on to his son, but the real pain of loss means that the rich man's offspring will receive nothing for all the effort that has been expended. This miserable prospect forces us to ask where the real values of life are. They certainly cannot be in money that can be lost so easily.

3. *A man should know who he is* (5:15–17)

The Teacher now offers a very meaningful observation. A person is born naked (v. 15); and, as the Jewish saying goes, his hands are grasping but there is nothing in them. When he leaves this life, his hands are folded over his chest; but there is still nothing in them. He may have had a fortune in his hands during his lifetime, but as he entered empty-handed, he leaves the same way—a sobering thought indeed!

"A sick evil" the Teacher exclaims in the midst of these considerations. If a person is interested only in money, what has he really labored for? He is toiling only for the wind, and what will be the gain (v. 16; see 1:3)? To toil for the wind is a picture of what is elusive and cannot be grasped. So again, what are the real values of life? To hang all of one's hopes on riches with the prospect of losing them? The end result of this kind of loss is only frustration, affliction, and anger. For most people who have lost fortunes due to bad business deals, their minds are taken up with those who have cheated them; their mental states become deranged. Is this what we live for in this world? What a waste! The Teacher could not have painted a more graphic description of those who make riches their goal. Even most unbelievers will see the wisdom of what he has to say concerning these meaningless pursuits in life.

4. Interlude: The way goods can be enjoyed (5:18–20)

The author here breaks into the assessment of life's difficulties and enables us to enter into the meaningful discoveries the Teacher has derived from his own experiences. The contrast of the miser's existence with the danger of losing his wealth leads us to realize a simple lesson in life: Material things can be enjoyed, a subject that the Teacher repeats from earlier statements (2:24 and 3:22). He realizes that what he would consider as good in this life is actually beautiful; we are to enjoy life in all our labor during the days of our lives on earth (v. 18). Life is a gift to be enjoyed, and God Himself provides it (v. 19). When God promised wealth and possessions, as was the case with Israel (Lev. 26:3–13; Deut. 28:1–14), He expected those gifts to be used in a right way and not hoarded or perverted to one's hurt. As man is absorbed in the task God gives him to do, the days will pass swiftly, and he will live with gladness of heart (v. 20). True, life has its frailties; but as a person lives in moderation, enjoying what this life can offer, he can be content. Who would not appreciate such an interlude that enables us to keep our sanity amidst the veil of tears in this world!

5. *One earns, another enjoys* (6:1–6)

The Teacher is not through with discussing this matter of money, and he brings us back again with a jolt to life's realities. He announces that he has seen or recognized an evil on this earth which "weighs heavily on men," literally "it is much upon men" (v. 1). The excruciating pain is that while God can give a man wealth, possessions, and honor (almost the same as what we see in 5:19), yet he will not have the opportunity to enjoy them. What kind of business is life from the human point of view whereby we are promised blessings on one hand and then have no possibility to enjoy what they afford? Life's experiences do not seem to work out the way they ought to!

Many are the ways by which a person is deprived of enjoying all that he has been privileged to acquire; it can happen through personal loss, already mentioned in 5:14; acts of war; or some form of violence. The point is that he is not able to enjoy his wealth, but instead some stranger will enjoy it (v. 2). The bitterness of tragedy is reflected by the word "stranger," suggesting that not even the heirs will receive the possessions but rather those with no just claim to them. The Teacher can only shake his head again at misfortune, all too prevalent in this life, and pronounce the whole business as meaninglessness and a sick evil. Such situations do not always happen, but they are a real possibility.

In still another description of sorrow, the Teacher depicts in Old Testament terms the blessings of numerous offspring (the figure of one hundred is exaggeration, Ps. 127:3–5) and living many years. But what a sad outlook on life if, after having received so many blessings, he still cannot enjoy his prosperity and, even worse, is deprived of a decent burial. The observation of such a state of affairs is that a stillborn child is better off than this unfortunate man. The classic illustration of such a person is Job who, after having tremendous wealth and many children, fell ill to a seeming incurable disease (Job. 3:11–16); and with no apparent prospect for recovery, he lamented as to why he ever saw the light of day!

Once the Teacher mentioned the stillborn child, he felt that he had to explain his statement (vv. 4–5). The stillborn child comes into the world with no purpose, no meaning; and it departs into darkness, that is, never seeing the sun and never really knowing anything. In traditional Jewish practice, such a child was not even given a name so that the event could be quickly put out of mind. This was done because this child never entered the experiences of the living—the joys and the meaningless evil of this life. The comparison becomes evident. The long life of a man who has had many children and many years and yet has not been able to enjoy them is contrasted with the stillborn child soon forgotten. But we find it difficult to understand the thinking of the Teacher on this score. Did not the man enjoy his children? Did he not also enjoy a wife with whom he had had relations through which many children were born? Yet there are many reasons why a person cannot enjoy prosperity; perhaps it is due to an illness, to deep depression, or to a disease that his wife or some of the children suffer from. We have to try to understand the lesson of the comparison. It would appear that no life, even as the stillborn, is preferable to a life in which all the good things cannot be enjoyed and which in the end brings dishonor with no proper burial.

We must not try to read the whole of Old or New Testament truth into the world view of the Teacher. For the believer there is certainly a life beyond this one, and there were expressions of this hope in the Old Testament (Ps. 23:6) as well as in the New (Phil. 1:23). But the Teacher was considering some real problems as viewed from this world instead of thinking of the blessings of the next world. Let us grant, says the Teacher, that this person unable to enjoy his prosperity was able to live as long as a thousand years twice over, more than double the age of Methuselah who lived the longest on record (Gen. 5:27). But the disadvantage is mentioned again; this person can, literally, enjoy no good, a strong phrase to emphasize how the one under observation is utterly removed from any good because of the many tragedies of life. It is true that prosperity cannot bring happiness.

After the discussion of being stillborn and dying a dishonorable death, the Teacher raises the question, "Do not all go to the same place?" Whether we are talking about an untimely birth or about a person who has lived a thousand years twice over, the end is still the same, that is, we all return to the dust (3:20). Has the wise man lost all hope whatsoever and become a total cynic? It would seem so. He probably has in mind that all must go through the same experience of being separated from an earthly existence. Certainly he is right when he suggests that this world is no place to rest in its ultimate and total sense. But again, if we are talking about life as we can observe it on this earth, we have to recognize the truth that both the joyless wealthy person and the stillborn child will die; and in that sense we will not find ultimate answers in this world. For most of us, it will be only as we wrestle with these difficulties in this world that we will come to realize that there is another world to consider and that there is a God who cares.

H. Life's Troublesome Questions (6:7–12)

A life without joy, even though a person has money, long life, and many children, can be quite a perplexing circumstance to try to explain; but now we are going to be faced with many unanswered questions with which we all struggle, believer as well as unbeliever.

Practically all of man's effort or toil is for his mouth, that is, the basics of life, a vivid commentary on the treadmill of life (v. 7). Most people get up early in the morning to go to work in order to earn enough to be able to just live. With the strength derived from this effort, people can keep on working so that in turn they can continue to live. Work and food become almost synonymous; and even though a person can enjoy both, we have to recognize that in the long run these basics have become the master of the man. But what of the appetite, literally soul, behind the mouth, or physical dimension? The soul of a man was designed to enjoy more than just mere basics of life, but too often spiritual expectancies are never realized. No amount of wealth can satisfy a person's inner being.

Perhaps we can see one of the problems of the joyless man with many children and long life; if his inner man has not been satisfied, prosperity in itself will be insufficient to care for genuine spiritual needs. When we think of the millions of people on this earth on a treadmill of existence, we as believers can begin to have an idea of the desperate needs of man's entire being. The Teacher himself had a sense of this need and therefore points out the real problem man faces when he lives for this world only.

Another seemingly unanswered question is the contrast between the wise man and the fool (v. 8), already mentioned in 2:15 and 16 where in the end both die. The problem then pertained to the advantage of wisdom. The Teacher now raises the question regarding the possessions of both the fool and the wise person. Does the wise man with his "advantage" of wealth know how to satisfy his soul better than does the fool? Conversely, does the poor man gain by knowing how to satisfy his own soul if he is able to handle himself well, both socially and morally before others (including the wise person)? Certainly the wise man may be better off than the fool because wisdom is considered more highly than is foolishness (2:13). But while the wise person may have more material things, he can be joyless and end up in a miserable way. On the other hand, the poor man has the same desires as the wise person; and true to his own nature, he desperately wants more than what he possesses. Therefore, it would appear that both rich and poor are no better off because their appetites, their very inner beings, remain unsatisfied. Such is the way of the people of this world. A poor drunk on a skid row once said to this writer that his wish was to have a million dollars, but three blocks away a wealthy and wise person could only cry because he had no inner satisfaction with life. Both had insatiable desires!

The Teacher seems to answer some of the questions already raised when he declares that the sight of the eyes is better than the wandering of the appetite, or soul (v. 9). At least it is possible to a certain extent to enjoy what we see or, better yet, to enjoy the present physical good than to contemplate the desire of the soul from within. The inner being of a person is never satisfied with what his life affords because the soul of a person must have other areas and other sources for its satisfaction. The believer will certainly understand the implacable and insatiable desire of the soul, even as the Teacher did. In his wisdom, he described accurately that the sense of satisfaction with physical, material things can in the long run only be meaningless and chasing after the wind.

The discussion now returns to a previous consideration (3:9ff.) that man is a mortal creature, locked into the confines of this earth (vv. 10–11). Prior to the Fall, man found his fellowship with God; but there is a barrier now between God and man, and man finds it difficult to have an essential satisfaction within him with the things of this life. These truths were considered already; and it becomes useless, therefore, to contend with God as to why He permitted the situation as it is. Job struggled with Him concerning his physical and mental state, but in his growth of wisdom he abandoned his questions of God's decisions. He arrived at the point where God wanted him because in his struggle with a joyless life, he learned how to trust God, and as a result his soul's desires were satisfied (Job 42:5–6). The natural man, however, continues to struggle; and he must learn that he lives in a world where one finds few answers except as he learns how to fear God and trust Him. The problem with mortal man is that the more he tries to figure out his quandary, based on what he can see, the more his inner being struggles with unfulfillment; and even words in the long run lose their meaning.

The string of unanswered questions seems to reach its climax (v. 12). Who knows what is good for man? Where can one find answers, particularly in a fleeting life as the years pass swiftly and, in most instances, in a context of suffering and meaningless existence? Who is the one to tell man what will happen after he leaves this life? Philosophers struggle with rationalizations as to what is the good and what will happen after this life. Various answers come and go, but they do not really satisfy everyone. The Teacher has accurately defined the world of the natural man. It is only when one realizes a world with no ultimate answers that he perhaps turns to God who alone can provide them. At this point, the reader is not told directly the ultimate answers and where one finds them. Perhaps the Teacher wants the reader to struggle with life's realities and then try to find the deeper answers that are discussed at a later point. Many times it is only in the crucible of life's bitter experiences that some will listen to what God has to say.

For Further Study

1. Describe one instance in your life when you knew you were helpless insofar as decision making was concerned and you felt God intervened.

2. Is it unsettling to you that the Teacher spent so much time discussing the here and now in the midst of the times of life? Why or why not?

3. How do you think the Teacher would answer the pacifist who feels that war is no option for any decent human being?

4. Do you think the Teacher's advice is to the point when we consider what we have stored away in our attics, basements, and garages?

5. Using a concordance, find the passages that state that God can love a person or nation and the circumstances in which love turns to hate. Try to discover what has brought about the change of attitude by God; then try to find how God's anger was turned back to love again.

6. From what was discussed in the section on time and eternity, how would you try to comfort an unsaved mother who has just lost her four-year-old son to leukemia?

7. List several examples from Scripture where God permitted men to make their wicked decisions and it seemed they would never be judged for their deeds.

8. Look in several Bible dictionaries to discover the meaning of a man's spirit, breath, and life from the Hebrew terms. Can you also see the similarities and differences between man and animals from these terms?

9. Using Bible dictionaries and theologies of the Old Testament, such as *Theology of the Old Testament* by G. Oehler and *Theology of the Older Testament* by J. B. Payne, find out the Old Testament teaching of immortality and subsequent judgment.

10. Six million Jewish people died in the holocaust. Can you point out a number of ways God intervened to bring about a change that lifted the burden of oppression?

11. Do you know any people who have suffered or are suffering for various reasons and wish they had never been born? Can they articulate their emotions to you as you seek to have a ministry of care and concern? If the person is not a believer, perhaps you will be able to share how our Lord also suffered for each one of us.

12. Discuss the difference between total dedication to God and a godly ambition of a Christian to be a successful business man. Is there or is there not a difference?

13. We have discussed the benefits of companionship in several levels of society where the individual can mature. Can there be at times a negative influence? If so, how?

14. List the various factors the Teacher describes that comprise worship.

15. In one or more Bible dictionaries, research the tax systems in the Old Testament as well as in Jesus' day under the Roman authorities.

16. Make a list of what the Teacher describes in 5:8–17 as the dangers involved in the search for, labor in, and time for money.

17. Using J. B. Payne's *Theology of the Older Testament* and A. B. Davidson's *Theology of the Old Testament*, research death in the Old Testament—how it came about, what was lost thereby, some aspects of suffering as a result, etc.

18. Can you find a number of instances where people in the Old Testament realized that the things of this life did not really satisfy and that only in the inner man and spirit can fulfillment be found? Job is obviously one example; were there others?

Chapter 4

How to Cope With Life
(Ecclesiastes 7:1–12:8)

The Teacher has just described a long list of harsh experiences in the reality of life's pursuits. At times he appears to give some ultimate answers to life where it is possible to find enjoyment as we live in moderation and as God provides opportunity to do so. Other times, some of the experiences he has described seem hopeless. But he is realistic and presents life as it is.

Now he continues his descriptions and experiences of life, but he also gives us the benefit of his experience in how to cope and live above the harsh realities and difficulties in which we sooner or later find ourselves. While some of his recommendations may seem strange, yet when we plumb the depth of his analyses, we find his suggestions will stand us in good stead.

A. What Is Considered the Better Activity (7:1–14)

The Teacher opens with a string of parables that catches our attention and points out what is better in life. He begins with a wise suggestion. One's name, to be understood as his reputation (Prov. 22:1), is better than the finest of perfumes, a reference to the perfumed oil used in the Middle East on joyful occasions (9:8; Amos 6:6; Song of Songs 1:3). It was of extreme importance—above many other considerations —that a person have the esteem of his contemporaries. As the perfumed oil gave an aroma that others noticed, so the influence of a person's reputation on others was better than perfume.

We are not quite prepared for the contrast in the second line of the proverb (v. 1b) that the day of departure from this life is preferable to our birthday. At first glance it seems strange to our western ears, but the two lines of poetry have a contrast from which we can learn much. The Teacher's technique at times is to jab us to keep us awake as he makes a startling statement and then provides his deductions. (See a similar situation in 4:9 and then the comment in 4:10–12.)

Delitzsch's suggestion that verse 1b is "not in the spirit of the Old Testament revelation of religion" (p. 313) might seem questionable. From what we have seen, the Teacher does have a wisdom that fits in quite well with the Old Testament literature, and his statements come from a wise observation of his own life's experiences. We must repeat again that he is no cynic or pessimist; he is merely stating things as they are.

Both Jewish and non-Jewish traditions have similar statements regarding a person's day of death. In Jewish literature there is the comment, "Do not trust in yourself until the day of your death" (Sayings of the Fathers 2:5); and the Midrash has a parable that teaches that men should not be joyful when a ship pulls out of the harbor to go to sea but instead rejoice when it returns after a safe voyage following the many storms. Interesting also is what Solon said to Croesus, "No man is to be counted happy until he has closed his life happily" (Gordis, p. 267, citing Heroditus 1, 32). The point seems to be well taken. It is not how well a person begins; rather, it is how well he ends, a positive outlook on 7:1b.

It is even more of a puzzle to try to understand why the Teacher suggests the more desirable activity of visiting the house of mourning instead of enjoying himself at the house of banqueting (literally, drinking; v. 2a, b). Jewish people did and still have a practice of observing a period of mourning when people die. In ancient Israel, upon the death of famous people, mourning took place for thirty days, divided into greater and lesser periods of seven and twenty-three days respectively. There also seemed to be some kind of a meal of comfort after the burial of the loved one (Jer. 16:7; Hos. 9:4).

The greater period of seven days is mentioned specifically in Ecclesiasticus 22:12, "Mourning for the dead lasts seven days." It was an honorable deed to visit the bereaved and sit with them for a period of time and comfort them.

But what is the point of seemingly spending more time in the house of mourning and with the bereaved than in pleasurable eating and drinking? The answer comes quickly that we have to face a sobering fact that death is the common end of all (v. 2c, d). We learn this experience all too soon when we visit those who have lost a loved one. Life's afflictions and sorrows do have more to teach us than the short periods of trying to escape from the pressures of life. We cannot shrug off these lessons because of what Moses taught us, "Teach us to number our days aright, that we may gain a heart of wisdom" (Ps. 90:12).

As the theme of mourning and death continues, we are reminded that sorrow is better than meaningless laughter with all of its clowning (v. 3a). The Teacher already had learned that laughter in itself was emptiness (2:1–2), but now he suggests that frivolity has to be tempered with a dimension in life that can teach us so much. Anyone who has lived long enough in the experiences of this world knows that sorrow deepens a person's maturity and puts rejoicing in its proper perspective. Paul seemed to catch this paradoxical lesson when he exclaimed that he was "sorrowful, yet always rejoicing" (2 Cor. 6:10).

The suggestion concerning the sad face as good for the heart (v. 3b) may seem to run counter to what has already been proclaimed, "A happy heart makes the face cheerful, but heartache crushes the spirit" (Prov. 15:13). On closer examination, however, the two statements of Ecclesiastes and Proverbs are not contradictory. The loss of a loved one, deep depression, and any other tragic experience can crush the spirit, and there seems to be no reason to even live. But many times it is just these experiences that give the deepest meaning to life when such an afflicted person begins to recover. It is the real knifing experiences of sorrow that put joy and cheerfulness in their proper perspectives. Literally, the phrase "good for the heart" is the "improvement of the heart," which reflects the maturing process. But the fool is empty-headed as he seeks for his fun in the escapes of life; what can he reflect from his heart?

The contrast continues as to what is better. Which of two houses does one resort to—the house of mourning or the house of pleasure (v. 4)? The wise person takes to heart the fact that he will learn the proper perspectives of life in the house of mourning, and this will influence the way he lives. Only the fool thinks that life is nothing more than an occasion for revelry and reckless living. Fools can laugh, but it is empty; and in the end the hilarity is stupid. The fool does not learn what life is all about!

The Teacher picks up another theme: Can we "take it" when the wise man rebukes us (vv. 5–6)? Many of the wisdom statements treat this topic. For example, "A wise son heeds his father's instruction" (Prov. 13:1); and "A rebuke impresses a man of discernment" (Prov. 17:10). In the teaching of wisdom by Israel's sages, particularly to the young and inexperienced, it was necessary to give instruction or discipline. The word "discipline" (Prov. 1:2; *musar*) is an emphasis that calls for firm correction to enable a person to follow a biblical moral as well as the ordering of his life in proper behavior. The word "rebuke" (7:5, *gearah*) refers to the earnest and severe word intended to impressively reprove. The Teacher uses it to warn us in his call to live wisely. We are encouraged by it to listen to the wise person's instructions for our own good.

But what of the fool? What does he have to offer us? The song of fools might be attractive. In the ancient world, as in the modern world, people sang songs to escape the problems of life. But most of the time these popular songs do not help a person to face reality; they are hollow, both spiritually and morally, and have nothing to offer except a bit of momentary entertainment.

The Teacher at one time had his fill of this entertainment and his assessment of the fool's songs is that they sound only like the crackling of thorns under the pot (v. 6). Cooking in ancient days took place outside of the house; and in order to sustain a fire long enough to produce the coals for warmth, the women used a log of wood that burned quietly for a long time. It would be ridiculous to use thorns that flare up quickly, crackle loudly, but soon exhaust themselves (Ps. 118:12). There is a play on words in Hebrew to make the point: the fool's song (*shir*), pot (*sir*), and thorns (*sirim*).

The lesson is well taken in the similarity of verses 5 and 6. As the thorns flare up quickly and noisily but soon die down, so is the song and laughter of the fool. Laughter rises quickly, but it also dies quickly; and when a person examines what was said for some comfort and help, the joke or song is completely meaningless. Shallow laughter is soon over and is of no aid to the person seeking answers to the real problems of life. The advice, therefore, is to avoid the meaningless lifestyle of the fool like the plague.

The discussion continues concerning fools and the wise person (v. 7). There seems to be a difficulty in seeing how verse 7 connects with the preceding two verses. Delitzsch suggests that a verse seems to be missing between verses 6 and 7 that would give it a smoother transition (p. 317), but this proposal does not suit the Teacher's style. He is given to making solitary statements to jar us and then adding some unconventional deduction of his own as we saw already (7:1).

It would appear that the startling declaration in 7:7 is a takeoff from the truth expressed in 7:5a. Even wise people can give way to their basest behavior, and the Teacher reminds us that they are not immune to the temptations of life. The word "extortion" ('osheq) is oppression in order to receive bribes, as explained in the parallelism in the second line of verse 7. It appears that no wise person would willingly make a fool of himself; but in the position of a judge, it is all too easy to take money or gifts extended under the table. Tragically, however, the prospects of easy money can even break down the inner resistance of the wise man who can twist justice and oppress poor people to receive this kind of bribe. The saying is true: Perfect power corrupts perfectly. The Teacher's appeal is to one's self-respect. For the wise person to pervert justice and become a corrupt ruler results in his becoming a fool; his understanding (literally, heart) will be corrupted and perish because it will be so twisted and perverted. The Teacher had seen enough examples of this failure and warns us accordingly that wisdom should not give way to foolishness. Why lose one's position of being considered wise and end up as a prattling fool who is accorded no respect whatsoever when he perverts himself?

Another series of proverbs teaches us the value of patience (vv. 8–9). The best way to grasp this lesson is to see life from a wide and full perspective. The Teacher has already led us to assess and learn from full-orbed experiences of sorrow as well as joy. So he repeats the point that the end of a matter is better than its beginning; therefore, we must learn how to be patient. After all, the experiences of life are to help us curb our impatience and to gracefully take things as they happen.

So why be proud? Proud of what? The reference to pride describes one haughty in his spirit, and in Proverbs we see almost the same construction of words whereby we are warned that a haughty spirit will lead to a downfall (Prov. 16:18b). A haughty person must learn that everyone and everything cannot be subservient to him. He has to learn to be quiet and grasp the lessons of life with patience; and in this way he will know that in the end he will be vindicated in his humility and openness of heart and mind.

Another dimension of a person with a haughty spirit is that he can be easily provoked (v. 9a). The Teacher warns each of us that we must learn how to control our spirits. The reference to spirit is interesting because in the Hebrew the spirit (*ruah*) "breathes quickly in animation or agitation" and can be equivalent to the temper or disposition (BDB, p. 925a, 3c). Jesus Himself was very pointed when He warned against people who are angry with others (Matt. 5:22).

The wise man knows how to be patient and control his anger and not be as the fool (v. 9b). Anger, or fretfulness, rests in the bosom of the fool; he is the one who cherishes and takes it to heart. By harboring a haughty spirit and fretfulness, a person loses his total balance with the issues of life and even his health. There is certainly a psychosomatic relationship between emotions and body functions. Only a fool has not learned how to contain himself and be patient, thereby hastening a breakdown in his physical well-being.

Still another attitude for a better approach to life is the consideration of discontentment with the present (v. 10). Perhaps the Teacher had a natural reason for moving from the fretful fool to the continual complaining about conditions as they are at present. There are always those who proclaim that "the good old days" were better; but these are only senseless words that can devastate and discourage people. A classic illustration of this attitude is when the foundations for the second temple were laid. Among the exiles who returned from Babylon were older people who remembered the Solomonic temple, and they complained that the second one would not have the same glory the former did in the "good old days" (Hag. 2:3). But there were Judeans present who were born in captivity with no memory of a past temple. The new temple with which they were involved in construction represented tremendous opportunities for them and their children. The point is that we live in the present and must always consider the opportunities it affords for our work which will last into the future. The Teacher can only assert that it is not wise, rather it is folly, to always be complaining about the present and looking back. We are encouraged to strive for what is best, avoid foolish things, look forward (v. 8a), be patient (vv. 8b, 9a), and ask for wisdom to have a healthy view on life (v. 10).

A classic epitome of what is better is to always seek for wisdom (vv. 11–12). We have been warned against the misuse of it (v. 10b) but now we will explore another dimension of wisdom. The Teacher already had his hurtful experience with it when he realized its meaninglessness if wisdom was to be the only goal of his life (1:17). However, he does not despise the right use of wisdom.

The translation "wisdom, like an inheritance, is a good thing" is well taken (v. 11a). Land inheritance in Israel was quite important. Each tribe and each family within the tribe had its apportioned part. If they suffered illness or other hardships, money could be obtained from the sale of the use of the land; the land however was not lost. In the year of Jubilee the land always reverted back to its original owners (Lev. 25:8ff.).

Wisdom also is a good possession and a blessing passed on to succeeding generations. Each generation had its sages who transmitted a godly wisdom based on a revelation of God. The wisdom literature in Israel sought to impart a lifestyle that touched every point of the round of life, and blessed indeed was the person who followed it. We have the benefits of wisdom today in the Word of God.

However, the Teacher has an objective to gain in this discussion, and he leads us along line by line. He observes that wisdom is a shelter even as money is a shelter; and there is a truth that the one who has wisdom and money will find himself in pleasant security (v. 12). Perhaps the picture comes from the Middle East where the sun beats down unmercifully in the heat of day, and people seek some kind of a shelter for protection. In the same way, money can provide protection from poverty and has its advantages in giving a person a measure of security. But the Teacher also hastens to say that wisdom is what affords protection by giving a person the means to live a godly lifestyle. The Teacher later speaks of a particular benefit of wisdom—a poor but wise man was able to save his city from an invading army (9:15).

It appears that there is an advantage (*yitron;* see 1:3) to knowledge (or wisdom) over money. Of the two, wisdom is the more desirable. Money can be lost, as we have indicated; or it can be taken by robbers. But who can rob a person of wisdom as long as he avoids the pitfalls of life and does not act as a fool (7:7)? Wisdom, and knowledge flowing from it, enables a person to see life in its broadest perspectives; guards him against being impatient, proud, or easily provoked; and always keeps him positive in his outlook. A man who has the protection of wisdom in this way will certainly have the best security in life.

As we view the situations of life, we will have many occasions to recognize that which is crooked, out of alignment, tangled, and in seeming total disorganization (v. 13). Is this not our lot even today? We too can view a world where so many things seem to go wrong. The Teacher, however, gently suggests that it will be only futile to go into a long discussion on God's permissive will. Ever since the days of the Fall, man, because of the quirk in his nature, has gotten himself into all kinds of difficulties. Will he in an ultimate sense straighten out the mess?

This act does not mean that no attempt should be made to rectify some of the more deplorable areas of life, but we have to recognize that no political or economic ideology will solve all the problems. In some situations, God bends or twists man's designs to either curb his evil or try to speak to him in his frustration.

The wisdom of the Teacher enables us to be joyful in times of prosperity, literally "in the day of good, be in good." Ecclesiasticus, in the period between the testaments, also reflects on this idea, "Do not deprive yourself of a happy day; let not your share of desired good pass by you" (14:14), a repetition of some of the statements already made that we are to enjoy the good things of life (2:24; 3:11). But what do we do when times are bad?

We are to perceive, or reflect, that both good and bad times are from God's hand. He has made the one as well as the other. Often there is a reason for bad times because God permits evil to come in order to serve His greater purpose. In His providential rule He can bring evil on a nation, and believers within that country must recognize His higher action. Thousands of people can be killed in natural disasters; individuals can fall prey to the worst of diseases. Obviously, there is a mystery in it all; and the believer does not have all-inclusive knowledge as God has. Who among men is able to foretell the future? Rather, we are told to be submissive to God and at the same time not to be excessively worried. Certainly for the believer this is good advice. But even the unbeliever has to recognize a factor over which he has no control. The Teacher has lived long enough to pass through the entire school of life and is able to impart his wisdom that we, too, may be triumphant even though we do not have the ultimate information God has concerning the entire picture of good and evil events. It is often in adversity that people find the Lord or believers are strengthened in their faith.

B. Dealing With Life's Excesses (7:15–22)

The previous string of proverbs in chapter 7 were designed to guide us into the better attitudes and activities in life. The Teacher now deals with the excesses in life and how people spend a lot of time talking about their injuries because of the excesses. He has had many opportunities to observe extremes that too often can be meaningless. His observation is that it is more profitable and desirable to find balance in the midst of life's extremes.

We note what appears to be, from an Old Testament point of view, an injustice: the righteous who perish in spite of their righteousness and the wicked who continue to live in spite of their evil acts (v. 15). This situation does not fit in with what had been promised Israel. David struggled with similar observations, namely, that the wicked prosper and the righteous are plagued (Ps. 73:3, 14). As we examine Leviticus 26 and Deuteronomy 28, we see that God promised Israel that the righteous will prosper in both body and spirit while the wicked will be cut down. But we see the jarring opposites here in 7:15, in Psalm 73, and in the unfortunate actions taken against Naboth who merely wanted to till his own land and live righteously before the Lord (1 Kings 21). These problems continue even to this day as seemingly good people die before their time while the wicked rich continue in their evil deeds, prospering all the while. We have to recognize that in the providence of God, He is sovereign and will in the end have His justice, vindicating the righteous and judging the wicked person. From this world's point of view, we do not have the whole picture as God sees it; and therefore, we have to be patient and realize that He knows what He is doing even if we do not.

The Teacher now considers the fact that people should not be over-righteous and overwise (v. 16)! On the surface we may wonder if he is serious; but on trying to think through what this wisdom writer is saying, we are forced to recognize the truth of his observations. If in many instances the righteous person perishes in spite of his righteous-ness (v. 15), then we might conclude that an excessive piety will not guarantee all that a person desires. The point is that we should not become *overconscientious* in what we can or cannot do. It is true that some people are so taken up with such perfection that there is little joy in living as a believer. And to what avail? In the end such a person can be cut down before his time. Being overrighteous can also mean that righteousness becomes distorted. A person can strain at the many externals of a righteousness that leads to legalism. We are warned, therefore, not to get caught up in this excess.

The Teacher continues his warning against striving to be overwise. He has already admitted that wisdom is better than folly (2:13) and money (7:12). But after a long discussion concerning the occasion when his sole interest was pursuing wisdom to the exclusion of everything else, he finally concluded that wisdom by itself can lead to much sorrow and grief (1:18). So he advises against being overwise and getting caught in the trap of the paradox that in seeking more and more wisdom, we can conclude only that there is an ever increasing area yet to know. In a word he is saying, "Don't overdo it!"

Interestingly enough, there is a reflexive to the verb "be overwise" (Hebrew *hithpael*). Accordingly, another translation is "make, or show yourself wise" (BDB, p. 314). The point is that a person should not think of himself wiser than he ought to or to think that he has some innate wisdom.

His final conclusion to being overrighteous and overwise is a question as to why a person should destroy himself. Certainly if overrighteousness and much wisdom become the sole goal in life, we only cut ourselves off from our family and friends and simply cannot relate to life. Even worse, we can suffer physical ailments that could cripple us and might even ensue in death.

Because the Teacher talked about being overrighteous and overwise, he also considers the opposites, being overwicked and a fool (v. 17). Once again, at first examination, we wonder whether we are advised that we may sin in moderation! But the believer recoils at such an intimation. Delitzsch seems to find the solution in "setting oneself free from the severity of the law" (p. 325) and suggests that overwickedness refers to the transgressions of the letter of the law and that we have to shake ourselves free from an overscrupulous conscience. While there may be some truth in the suggestion, there are other factors to consider.

The attempt by Delitzsch to understand "not be overwicked" is to substitute for it the alternative phrase "nor over 'sin'" *(teheta')*. But this change is an impossibility because we are not to sin! However, Delitzsch's technique helps us to grasp what the Teacher is getting at. We are not to deliberately sin. Rather, we are told not to be overrighteous, that is, to get caught up with an overconscientousness or a legalistic righteousness (v. 16a); then perhaps in parallelism we have to curb as much as possible what we are capable of in wickedness.

Man has a sin nature, and the believer certainly recognizes this sad fact when he often does stray. Even unbelievers realize often the lurking quirk in their being that does not enable them to reach their goal. So how do we control this nature that we ruefully realize? One aspect of true wisdom is to stand in reverential awe before God (v. 18; Prov.

1:7a); in fact, this is the way by which we begin to apprehend God and know that He cares for us. Therefore, as we receive wisdom from Him to live godly in this life, we will begin to discover the power to help us restrain as much as possible the practice of making wrong choices. We will discuss the truth of verse 20 shortly, but some of it is already in mind in verse 17. The point is well taken therefore. A person is not to be overstrict in his righteousness, but at the same time he must not give way to what the human nature desires in wickedness and become a fool (ṣakal).

The word for fool usually refers to the person who is in the habit of making questionable and wrong moral and spiritual choices. To place oneself above the Word and its discipline only introduces the question, "Why die before your time?" (v. 17b, c). This is an interesting point because the Teacher had indicated previously that a man's time to die is already fixed (3:2a), but we must temper this statement by the particulars and face the fact that a person can die an untimely death if he makes a practice of pursuing evil. There are many examples in the Mosaic constitution that called for the death penalty which cuts a person's life short; for example, a son who blasphemes his parents (Lev. 24:10ff.) and numerous moral improprieties (Lev. 20). Even the New Testament brings out the horrifying fact that believers can die before their time if they will not judge their unrighteousness, "a number of you have fallen asleep" (1 Cor. 11:30). The warning is therefore well taken; if a person is wise, he will respect the moral admonitions of the Word to curb the immoral propensities of a fallen nature.

We are finally told in verse 18 that it is good to grasp "the one," that is, the counsel of verse 16 in not being overconscientious and a full-blown perfectionist; neither should we let go of the other (v. 17), literally, not "resting your hand" from giving human nature full rein. With these double influences in our lives, we are encouraged to avoid the harmful extremes of two activities in life. We will be able to do so as we fear God, that is, stand in reverential awe before Him.

The Hebrew word translated "avoid" is "to go forth" (v. 18); in a number of instances it also can mean "he has fulfilled his obligation" (Berakot 2:1) and "'he has discharged' his duty" (the Mishnah). Therefore, the idea of "avoid" is derived from what is accomplished and, in the context, relates to avoiding the extremes and finding the balance between them.

The fear of the Lord is the link to wisdom (Ps. 111:10; Prov. 1:7), and it is with wisdom that we can have a restraint on extremes. But in another way, wisdom is a dire necessity in government (v. 19). (How well we know this truth after seeing what passes for wisdom in different bodies of government!) Towns and cities need protection in time of war. On other occasions, protective measures are a dire necessity; for example, when law and order is about to break down, when there is the threat of a loss in trade, or when a disease spreads. While city rulers often represent the best types of people, nevertheless there is always the need for the wise person who can give advice on how to avoid danger and many other threatening problems. A wise man is therefore not only a prominent but also a powerful figure who is valued for his good sense to counter the emergencies a society faces.

From what has already been discussed concerning excesses—not being overrighteous or overwicked, finding the balance of not being overwise and yet praising wisdom—the Teacher now makes a confession to which all of us will have to agree (v. 20). This verse begins with a connective usually translated "for" and therefore suggests the connection between this verse and what has immediately preceded it.

While it would not appear that the doctrine of man's moral depravity is set forth, yet all of us have to confess that we do fail to attain the ideal of being righteous. There is a shorter statement of this truth offered in the prayer at the time when Solomon's temple was being dedicated, "for there is no one who does not sin" (1 Kings 8:46).

It would be a mistake to consider this verse as saying that there are no righteous people on earth. In the Old Testament often the believer was called the righteous person, not because of his self-effort but because he believed the truths of God set forth in His revelation and was declared righteous, that is, justified. Abraham was declared righteous (Gen. 15:6), and many times the psalmist also spoke of believers as righteous (Pss. 11:7; 37:30; 64:10; 112:6). The Old Testament generally underscores the *results* of an atonement whereby a person lives a righteous life. The New Testament emphasizes the *means* of atonement, that is, belief. Obviously, we also see the requirement of belief in the Old Testament as well as the necessity for the righteous lifestyle of the believer in the New.

The point, however, is that even a righteous person, a believer, while doing what is right, often will discover that he "misses the mark," that is, misses the moral goal toward which he is aiming. Wrongdoing occurs often when a believer avoids a godly wisdom to prevent it. The only power that will keep a man from going down to destruction or guard him from committing transgression is the wisdom that comes from God as we learn how to reverence Him. The attainment of this wisdom is good advice to the unbeliever, but it is an absolute necessity for the believer in order to curb his old sinful nature that will be ever present until he leaves this life. This wisdom is enough to keep us humble before the Lord so that we do not fall into temptation; but with the wisdom He gives, we can continue on the narrow road through life that leads to His presence.

To prove his point, the Teacher demonstrates how, in one instance, wisdom can help us avoid pitfalls (vv. 21–22). We are admonished not to listen too closely (literally, give our hearts) to everything people say about us. Instead of gloating in the commendation we expect from others, we could hear people speak very unkindly of us at times. But why? As we reflect on what is being said, we have to realize that even we believers have fallen into the same trap of speaking ill of others; and the truth of verse 20 then comes home to us with great force! Our employees could also have good reason to speak ill of us because we have done wrong. But on the other hand, we do the same; we condemn others because we have seen them do wrong and are quick to criticize. Therefore, as we humbly recognize the truth of verse 20 we have to acknowledge the need for balance, not becoming overrighteous so as to pick on the faults of others, because we fail too and then others condemn our acts of wrongdoing. May God keep us ever humble and help us to know our true nature and therefore lean hard on Him and rely on His wisdom!

C. How Much Can We Really Know? (7:23–8:1)

As the Teacher pauses after looking back at what he has declared in the past several verses about finding a balance between excesses and acknowledging that wisdom is better (7:12, 19), he has to admit that he has not attained an ultimate wisdom. He has examined a number of specific instances where wisdom has taught him well, but like Job (28:12ff.), he continues searching for fundamental wisdom in spite of life's limitations. All who are sensitive to the will of God recognize this endeavor amidst life's pressures and joys to find ultimate answers. But unbelievers likewise struggle with the same difficulties in seeking basic wisdom and answers to life.

The Teacher begins with "all this" (v. 23); he perhaps was referring

to the rules of conduct already discussed in chapter 7, but there is also
a sharp anticipation of what he wants to learn concerning a fundamental
wisdom. With his declaration, "I tested by wisdom," he continues with
his honest search to find out the essence of things that are. Previously
he declared that men "cannot fathom what God has done from beginning to end" (3:11), but this fact does not hinder him as he continues to
look, even as we do in our day. He insists that "I am determined to be
wise," that is, he wants to fully know this basic wisdom so he can
explain the mysteries of time and answer questions that trouble mankind. But he has to admit that what he is searching for always seems so
elusive. He learns some facets of wisdom but does not attain its fundamental aspect.

The Teacher is not questioning the fact that ultimate wisdom actually
exists; he is sure that this wisdom has being (v. 24). However, he must
confess that it is far off in its ultimate sense and very deep, a Hebrew
compound that emphasizes it in a superlative way. He raises the question concerning who can reach it, discover it, in an intellectual sense.
In many ways he is a wisdom teacher, but he discovers his limitations
to find the essence of wisdom even though he can teach a number of
specific, concrete lessons.

All this discussion is only a general observation concerning what we
can know, but the Teacher does have something specific in mind about
this matter of fundamental wisdom (v. 25). He turns his mind (Hebrew,
heart; see 2:20 for a similar occasion of turning) to a number of areas of
investigation. With his whole heart he wants to be involved in his
search and not do it in a superficial manner. His deepest desire is to
understand (know) in an intellectual sense, to investigate (explore), and
to search out (seek out) wisdom and the scheme (explanation) of things.
He has dedicated himself to a careful study and will not be deterred.
He is involved in a noble effort.

In addition the Teacher also wants to understand (know) the stupidity of wickedness. The reference to wickedness describes the choices
that lead a person to turn away from God and from the Word that is
designed to teach him to do good. A lifestyle of wickedness is stupid,
and the person who makes the wrong choices hates knowledge (Prov.
1:22), takes no pleasure in understanding (Prov. 18:2), and finds pleasure in evil conduct (Prov. 10:23). In his search for knowledge the
Teacher also seeks to discover the horror of the madness of folly.
Interestingly, folly comes from the same verb as stupidity; once again

we see how folly, or stupidity, is sheer madness and causes ungodly men to be blind to wisdom and to rage in their wicked behavior. But how can we know in an ultimate sense, and do we even want to know, all the ways of wickedness and folly man takes?

With these specific questions, was the Teacher able to attain to ultimate wisdom? No. His answers provide only the particulars of knowledge, but they are very important because they will lead him to discern between good and evil. He does not completely despair in his search since he at least is finding out pertinent and extremely useful information. The effort expended in his search for wisdom will help him build a fund of knowledge to make even more helpful pronouncements for a godly lifestyle.

The Teacher describes the woman who ensnares man (v. 26) but goes even further to declare that he has not found one upright woman among a thousand (v. 28)! From today's viewpoint the implications are devastating. Does he mean to say that not one good woman can be found? If this is his thought, then he is in trouble with many of our women's movements today! Various explanations have been offered to avoid these implications: 1) the woman spoken of in deprecation is heathen philosophy that detracts from the real wisdom (Leupold, p. 173); and 2) the woman, and man who also falls short (v. 29), is interpreted to be civilization at large (Gordis, p. 283). As difficult as the text is, we have to probe it for the real meaning.

The Teacher found an experience more bitter than death (v. 26). What is it that could be worse than the heartwrenching experience of the death of a loved one or close friend? It is the woman who is a snare, the same word used for the hunting net in which birds are caught (9:12) and huge siegeworks used for blockading (9:14). Why should a woman be described in this sense, and what had she done for men to be warned to keep away from her?

The woman under consideration has a heart like a trap or fishing net in which her victims are caught; her hands are like chains, holding her victim as a prisoner with vice-like clutches. When we are later told that the man who pleases God will escape from her, we are not left to imagine too much as to what is in mind. The wisdom of Proverbs 5 is reflected here where two women are contrasted—the legitimate wife and the adulterous woman. In Proverbs 7 wisdom is the true sister while the adulteress is to be avoided like the plague. It appears without question that the wise man is talking about the loose woman who can take hold of the unsuspecting man and entrap him (Prov. 7:13). The Teacher clearly warns that if a man holds God as the object of his love, then he will escape the adulteress. The sheltering hands of a loving God are more to be desired than all the illicit love in this world.

However, the Teacher is not content to leave the matter. He emphasizes the point that we should look with him, see, and understand well what he has discovered (vv. 27–29). We started out in verse 23 by observing that the Teacher wanted with all his heart to know ultimate wisdom and continued to add one thing to another to discover or find out the scheme of things, that is, a well-grounded and established knowledge. While he indicates that he is not able to find this ultimate knowledge, he does get into a discussion concerning what can be disagreeable to men and women. He found only one upright man among a thousand, but not one woman was among the same number! Is he saying this with tongue in cheek? Certainly he does respect a wife when he tells a man to "enjoy life with your wife, whom you love" (9:9), and he has only praise for marital fidelity with no questions raised regarding the wife. In Proverbs the wise Teacher praises the wife in many ways (i.e., 12:4; 14:1; 18:22; 19:14; 31:10–31).

Taking the focus off the woman for the moment, the search among a thousand human beings could reveal only one man as he *ought to be*. (The word "upright" does not appear in the Hebrew text.) The point is that the Teacher was looking for the ideal, righteous, wise person who might serve as his model; but the search was disheartening.

Why, however, in the search among an equal number of people, could there not be found a woman who could fit the model of the ideal, righteous, and wise? (Again, the words "one" and "upright" concerning the woman are not in the Hebrew text.) We might ask, "Where was the Teacher looking?" If he was searching among his harem (700 wives and 300 concubines, 1 Kings 11:3), it is doubtful that he would find a woman as she ought to be among the pagan women who had turned his heart from God. Unacceptable also is the view that because no ideal woman could be found among a thousand, therefore not one woman was honored to author a book of the Bible, a task given only to the chosen few among men. Neither is it fair to throw in a crumb to say that certain godly women have written sacred songs in Scripture—Miriam, Deborah, Hannah, and Mary (Leupold, p. 177). This position seems so unfair, but we are still left with the problem as to why he *seemingly* deprecated the woman.

Perhaps it is safest to say that since he has in only rare moments found an ideal righteous man searching for ultimate wisdom, and even fewer women, that he therefore proceeds to his final observation. He introduces his conclusion with "this only have I found" (v. 29). He states that God made mankind, or the world of all human beings, upright. Adam *and* Eve, both human, were made originally upright in a state of innocence. After the Fall, mankind was characterized by a fallen nature but not totally unaware of the difference between good and evil. Both a man and a woman, because of their common fallen nature, can make wrong moral choices and indulge in sinful practices. With this nature both often exhibit how far they have strayed from the ideal.

In considering biblical history, however, it was Eve who tempted man to sin, being the first to be deceived, and then enticing her husband to follow her choices. In the pronouncements by God concerning Adam and Eve after the Fall, both of them are under the curse. Eve, and all women afterward, are to bring forth their children in pain. Man is to earn his food and whatever else by the sweat on his brow (Gen. 3:16, 19). But God did add a further restriction concerning the woman in that she is to serve her husband, and the husband is to exercise rulership over his wife. In no way does this deprecate the woman because she can provide as much input within the family relationship as she desires, but in the headship the man has his responsibility to exercise the leadership in the family.

In the ancient world, among pagan nations and even from selected sources in the Jewish traditions, the fundamental makeup of a woman with her desires and actions was not held in high esteem; and it was deplorable if the woman asserted any kind of leadership, such as Vashti's action in the Persian court (Esth. 1:17b). The Teacher does not go as far as this statement; but perhaps he somehow, because of the pronouncements by God after the Fall, reflected generally the concern of headship whereby man is to take the leadership in matters of the spiritual realm. This fact does not mean that in specific instances a woman cannot be wise so as to provide acceptable advice and expertise in many areas in both the family and society. But the role of the wise and ideal teacher will be in areas of spiritual leadership, and therefore we see the guidance in 7:28.

The Teacher has had a long, hard struggle with the problem of attaining the essence of wisdom (8:1). In his long experience he also

indicated the futility of making this search the *only* goal of his life
(1:12ff.). But he has learned already in his search for ultimate wisdom
that there is no one who can equal the wise man, and no one likewise
can know or understand the explanation or foundation of things like the
wise person. He is not being one-sided, but he has lived long enough
to realize that a godly wisdom is indispensable to "make it" in this
world and to get at the "whys" of so many of life's experiences.

The last two lines of verse 1 are a popular proverb indicating what
wisdom from God and His Word can do for a person when he takes it to
heart. His face is brightened, even as the psalmist declared in Psalm
119:130 and 19:8; the gloom is taken away; and joy and peace are very
evident on the countenance. The fourth line of the verse follows as a
matter of course whereby godly wisdom takes away a man's hard appearance. The word "hard" is rendered "impudent" in BDB (p. 739),
but here the meaning is reflected by the description of the "fierce-
looking nation" (Deut. 28:50) or the "stern-faced king" (Dan. 8:23). The
entrance of godly wisdom has the power to change the hard appearance
of a person's face and make it shine with the glory of God; and only a
believer can know this experience firsthand. As a result, he finds life
and receives favor from the Lord (Prov. 8:35). Certainly we are not
talking about mere intellectual wisdom but that which comes from
God, enabling a person to become a believer when he learns to fear the
Lord.

While the Teacher has not arrived with an ultimate wisdom, yet he
does not give up on acquiring its specifics that enable him to live in the
push and pull of everyday life. As he piles up the specifics, perhaps the
real essence of wisdom will be revealed.

D. Submit to the King (8:2–9)

The Teacher in the ancient world was just as much concerned with
an individual's relationship to the state as we are in our world today.
How does a person relate to the rulers of a country, particularly when
the government is not a democracy? Believers in the West have tasted
freedom for so long that it appears almost impossible to live godly in
any other type of government. What we must recognize is that believers down through the centuries have had to live for the Lord under the
worst possible kinds of governments and with the most capricious and
tyrannical rulers as one can imagine. Wisdom then can give us light as
to how to relate to the state.

We are provided with timely advice to obey the king's command or submit to the ruling authorities (v. 2). What a declaration in a day when terrorism reigns supreme and there is no respect for government! Although the phrase "I say," reflecting the verb "to say," is not in the text, yet it is to be understood as such; and, because the Teacher himself is a king, his "I say" or "I declare" is very apropos. The call to submission is also reflected by Paul who reminds us to submit to the authorities (Rom. 13:5).

The oath that was taken before God lent support to the need for submission to the government and its king in ancient Israel. The oath of obligation was a promise to God by the people to be faithful to their king and to give him their allegiance; at the same time the king declared that he would be faithful to his subjects. The promises were given not merely on the human level because God is the ultimate of kings and is the real King in the theocracy; a promise to Him to be faithful was also a pledge to the king of Israel who ruled as God's regent. Note such incidents in the Old Testament (2 Sam. 5:3; 2 Kings 11:17). We can therefore see the importance of what Paul said in Romans 13:14.

Somewhat the same procedure took place in many of the rituals of ancient pagan nations. In a sense, treaties were made between a king and his subjects; but there was also the national god who stood behind the earthly kings. People yielded their allegiance to their king but in a real sense recognized the power behind the king.

Because of the promises to the king and God, a person must not be in a hurry to leave his presence (v. 3). (Although "king" is not in the Hebrew text, this word is apropos.) The Teacher has discussed already why a person should not be hasty in other ways (5:2; 7:9), but here the warning is not to be impulsive so as to withdraw an allegiance merely because the king said something displeasing. The idea of rebelling or leaving our post is seen in 10:4 and Hosea 11:2, but wisdom helps us to restrain ourselves in the presence of rulers.

What bad cause are we warned about not standing up for (v. 3)? The sense of the text suggests that a person is not to even enter into or begin to engage in a conspiracy that could turn out badly. Another possibility of understanding the phrase is that a person does not stand against an evil word of the king, that is, does not hesitate doing what the king says even though his order is morally wrong. Those who choose this position say that no one can countermand the king since he can do whatever he pleases. It would seem that the first position is correct. There are times when we know that the word and action of a king is not right, but there must be the appropriate time to act against the king's wish. We shall discuss this matter further when we come to verse 6.

The king's word is supreme or powerful (v. 4). Almost the same terminology is expressed concerning God (Job 9:12; Dan. 4:32; Wisdom of Solomon 12:12), suggesting that the king's rulership has been given to him by God Himself. Paul also reflects this statement (Rom. 13:14). It is also interesting that the word "supreme," that is, ruler, can be a predicate nominative where ruler stands equivalent to king. Therefore, we recognize that the word that goes forth from the king is as if it is the king. Something similar takes place when God speaks His words. When He blessed Israel and set them apart, Balaam could not curse Israel; instead, Balaam's words were turned around to be equivalent to that which God had already spoken concerning Israel. How, therefore, can anyone take an opposing position and question the words of the king? In this sense, we recognize today that since God has delegated His authority to the state, anarchy is an ideology that is totally out of the question.

The king's commandment demands respect and obedience, even at times when it is despotic (v. 5). Obeying the commands of the king and the laws of the state will, in a general sense, not bring harm to the citizen. The wise man takes it to heart that in the face of oppression by the king or the state, there will be the time when God will interpose. When that propitious moment comes, there will then be the opportunity to deal with oppression. This fact reminds us again of the Teacher's emphasis on a time for everything and the reality that we live in an ever-changing world. When a king becomes oppressive or a state's decisions and actions become immoral, we know that these situations will not go on forever. God is really in control of governments, and the wise person knows God has a time for judgment and therefore will not enter into a premature rebellion where the outcome will be devastating.

This discussion continues in verse 6 and reminds us again of the need for the use of prudence in any political or military action regarding an oppressive king or state. Meanwhile, as the wise man waits judiciously, he and others suffer in misery. Wickedness weighs heavily on him as he sees despotic kings become even more cruel. Waiting can be excruciating at times until the right moment comes to protest against evil decisions.

There are times when we will act in peaceful protest when a ruler or government becomes immoral. Daniel and his three companions did not have to wait too long; the right moment came when they could no longer obey King Nebuchadnezzar as to who was to be worshiped. But what about other occasions when we cannot wait as a government violates the sanctity of life? Could real believers wait apathetically when the National Socialist government of Germany issued its decree to kill all Jewish people? Many Christians were not apathetic and felt that no government has the right to take away a person's life because of who he is; therefore, many became engaged in an action of justice to hide Jews.

We recognize the general truth that the authority of the state has God's stamp of approval on it. There are conditions, however, when it is difficult to determine the timing at which point God's justice begins to act and a wise person realizes he has to begin a resistance. When does a Martin Luther King mount a resistance to social customs of a society that degraded the black man? When should black Christians begin some kind of action with an apartheid government?

The Teacher seems to have this difficult thought in mind concerning some aspect of political action with immoral governments as he continues his discussion. It is only a matter of the right time when God will act to judge repressive regimes and punish evil rulers, and nothing will hinder His action (vv. 7–8). But the discussion also deals with more general truth. No man, or no one (in the Hebrew text "man" does not appear), knows the future. Some might say verse 7a refers to the unpredictability of how long tyrant rulers will continue in office, a thought that is certainly in the picture; but the intent of the verse should be left in more general terms. The despot does not know what faces him and how he will end, and neither does the wise man know just at what moment or exactly how the intolerable wicked situation will come to a conclusion. All mortals grope as they try to find answers in the midst of earth's wicked circumstances.

Wickedness eventually will be restrained. Does man have power over the wind to restrain it (v. 8)? The Hebrew word for wind is *ruah* or spirit. An evil tyrant could have power over his spirit but not over the wind. This is a prerogative that belongs to the sphere of God's control (Prov. 30:4). Does anyone have power over the day of his death? The

Hebrew word for power is the same as "supreme" or rule in verse 4. Therefore, we understand that no man possesses the rule, or is a ruler, over death because he is not able to calculate when it will occur in order to change the day. That date is in the hand of God. Can anyone be discharged, or given some special dispensation, during the course of war? If a person's country is in mortal danger, it is understandable that discharges would be out of the question.

In conclusion, therefore, the Teacher insists that because of these three impossibilities (no power over the wind, day of death; or discharge during war), wickedness will not release those who practice it. No evil schemes will save a tyrant from death or an immoral government from punishment. Wickedness eventually leads to disaster; in the long run evildoing does not succeed. We learn that the general rule, therefore, is to be obedient to the state. At the same time, however, when a government becomes immoral and an evil tyrant, there is a providential rule of God that sooner or later curbs evil. The wise man, or believer, will often have to be patient and watch for the opportune time when God begins to act. But there will be those times when man acts in resistance to the state within the will of God.

The concluding statement on royal power, and the power of the state from our viewpoint today, is offered by the Teacher who has lived long enough to observe carefully what happens all too frequently to many kings and rulers (v. 9). Rulers come and go, and most never learn from the experience that wisdom wants to teach. Kings may start out well, a government at its inception may have the interests of its subjects at heart; but sooner or later the line of propriety is crossed and rulers become tyrannical. In the long run, rulers hurt themselves and are cut off suddenly because of the wickedness they perpetrate on innocent people. How tragic that the tyrannical rulers of today never seem to learn from past history!

E. On Being Warned of a Mixed-up Sense of Justice (8:10–14)

The Teacher returns to the subject of the actions by the righteous and the unrighteous (cf. 7:15). He declares in a matter-of-fact way that retribution concerning the wicked can be delayed and therefore justice becomes mixed up and turned around. Such situations cause him to lament, but he faces the hard facts of reality. Of course, evil will not always triumph (7:17, 25; 8:8d), and he warns against a life of wickedness (7:17f.).

This wise man is not blind to the fact that the values of justice and righteousness can become shallow in a complacent society. For example, the day comes when the wicked die and are buried (v. 10). The tragedy, however, is that these very people—evil as they were—used to come to and go from the holy place, the Temple itself, and were honored and praised by the religious leaders themselves. Does this ever happen? Of course! Certainly the Teacher had seen the tyrants and despots of his day who had the blessing of the nation's religious leaders and the praise of some people. How can God's moral remain pure when dishonest and evil people live as they do? How can religious leaders remain sensitive to a moral when they bless the wicked? And how can people, because they have derived money and other advantages from evil sources, praise the wicked? When the Teacher has to think of twisted morals, he cries out that this mixed-up sense of justice is meaningless.

As in our day, so it happened in the Teacher's day that the sentence on the wicked was delayed again and again (v. 11). They were protected while their victims were forgotten. Justice is gravely miscarried when sentences are perverted, delayed, and even set aside. When justice was delayed long enough, crimes were forgotten. The result only encouraged other evildoers whose hearts were filled with schemes to do wrong and who thought they could get away with it. Times have not changed; we do not seem to learn from the past!

The Teacher expresses his faith in the judgment process of God that man's mixed-up sense of justice will not prevail in the long run (vv. 12–13; cf. 8:8d; 7:17c). He had lived long enough to see the wicked prosper and commit a hundred crimes, but godly wisdom advises that when a person fears, is reverent, before God, his cause always will be upheld by the divine King. On the other hand, because the wicked do not fear God, they are only fools (Prov. 1:7), and it will not go well with them. Even though they live long enough to commit the hundred crimes (a number of exaggeration to describe a really evil character), they cannot lengthen their days like a shadow, that is, prolong their lives. There just might be the hint of an afterlife where, if justice is not carried out in this world, the great leveler will come and the wicked will be separated from the righteous and suffer while the righteous will be comforted. (See Pss. 49:14, 15; 73:18ff.) The Teacher expresses his hope and trust in God and calls on other people to fear and trust in Him likewise. While the problem is not completely solved concerning the evils in life, yet there is some hope offered to victims of crime if they trust in the righteous King who will vindicate them.

The nonsense continues, however, with the observation that because of a maddening, mixed-up sense of justice in this world, the righteous can get what the wicked deserve; and conversely, the blessing of the righteous is conferred on the wicked (v. 14). Wicked rulers know how to protect their own interests, and what should have been judgment on evildoers is passed off to innocent bystanders.

There is another factor to consider, however, as to why evil and wickedness are permitted to exist. Sometimes in His providential rule, God gives time for rulers and judges to make decisions and carry out their ideas whereby all that is present in their evil hearts becomes visible for everyone to see. But within this ongoing process, righteous believers often are caught in it and suffer. Many a believer has been hurt and even died while rulers apparently have gone scot-free and are living well. Who can even begin to figure out all the meaningless injustices that have ever happened on earth? The Teacher in his wisdom is aware that there are facets of knowledge with which he struggles. How long does it take for a ruler's crimes to become evident and the righteous vindicated? He does realize that God's time of retribution will always come, but if it does not take place here on earth, there is an ultimate rectifying of a perverted justice.

F. An Interlude: Enjoy Life in Spite of Problems (8:15)

Once again there is an interlude in the midst of difficult realities with the theme of trying to enjoy life as much as possible (3:12, 22; 5:18). But if justice can be miscarried, how in the world can people enjoy themselves? Yet as long as we live in this world, and this is the world in which we do find ourselves, then we ought to learn how to live in spite of injustices, trust God, and take the blessings that have been provided for us and eat, drink, and be glad. For both believers and unbelievers, this is good advice of what we shall yet say in verses 16–17. The darker side of life is ever with us, but we cannot become morbid because there are also the joys as we work during the days of our lifetime. There has to be a balance between misery and happiness, but we cannot ever overlook the happiness. God can let us have satisfaction from our toils where meaning and purpose can be enjoyed, and many times these joyful interludes of life are what make it bearable in the midst of suffering and horror.

G. Trying to Solve Life's Riddles (8:16–17)

A number of life's troublesome questions have already been discussed (6:7–12), but the Teacher returns to the attempt to understand some of these riddles with a wisdom that will enable us to live above them. He musters all of the wisdom at his command to view man's labor here on earth; his heart is very much involved in his search, "his eyes not seeing sleep day or night" (v. 16). And what is his assessment after viewing man involved with his restless labor and observing all God has done and is doing in this world, that is, His government and ultimate responsibility for the things on earth (v. 17)? If a person is trying to discover ultimate meaning and wisdom from the vantage point of this world, then it is a self-defeating task. Even the wise man includes himself among this group; he admits that he cannot fully comprehend or ascertain all of God's plans. Another wise man, Job, also cried out, "Where can wisdom be found?" (Job 28:12) in his search for it and concluded, "the fear of the Lord—that is wisdom" (Job 28:28). Both believer and unbeliever can agree on this point. All we can discover are the particulars of wisdom as the Teacher already admitted in trying to find ultimate wisdom (7:23ff.). But these particulars encourage us to rest assured that God has a plan that involves everything that happens even though He has not chosen to reveal the totality of it to every person, even the wisest. Philosophers have struggled with the meaning of this world; and while they have discovered some facets of it, yet even they must confess that they have not reached their goal. But this is God's world, and the wise believer can take some comfort in this fact and trust the divine King who stands behind His plan. We will have to content ourselves with the reality that all of life's riddles are not solved in this world as we presently know it.

H. Death Comes to All, but We Must Live (9:1–10)

1. *Do we dare talk about death?* (9:1–6)

Death! People have different ways of handling this experience— morbid curiosity, downright frustration, abhorrence with a facial grimace, unwillingness to even think about it. But we have to face the little we know about it from the vantage of life's ups and downs, the loves and hates of this world, the presence of wickedness while the righteous suffer, etc.

The Teacher previously described the difficulty of getting at total knowledge in this life (8:17); but now he takes it to heart and concludes, that is, sifts and winnows, some further information of which he has no complete knowledge (v. 1). He understands that the righteous and the wise (or the believer) have a specific lifestyle in which their deeds are in the hands of God (Ps. 31:15; Prov. 21:2). As believers trust God and do His will, they—as well as their deeds—are conditioned by God who governs this world. This much the Teacher was able to ascertain. While we do not have total knowledge of what occurs within the plan of God, yet of some aspects of the plan we are sure; and of that we do not know, we have to trust God that He knows what He is doing in His world.

But now we see one aspect of the inability of getting at this total knowledge from this world's viewpoint. Will the actions of the pious and wise earn for them God's love, or will they suffer? We need to remember that we are not talking about the afterlife and what awaits us in God's presence. The sphere of consideration is this earth and the experiences that await the believer as he makes the decisions he feels God wants him to make. But then what happens to him after he has exercised his moral choices to do the right thing? When the godly person suffers because of uncontrolled circumstances, does he then conclude that God does not favor him? Or course, we are supposed to trust God no matter what the circumstances are; but we are human, as the Teacher points out so eloquently. At times we are sure of God's favor and love, but other times we ponder and sometimes even seriously question. In the real world, there are times of oppression, personal loss, and even crippling diseases that the believer suffers. Even Job wondered what was happening to him as he sat on the edge of town, covered with loathsome sores while his three "friends" lectured him concerning his sins that brought on his disease. Yet his faith matured in his trials, and he can comfort us. Hosea lost his wife and suffered deeply although he learned from his own loneliness how God was lonely when His people had forsaken Him. Even Jesus suffered and learned obedience as a result (Heb. 5:7–8); yet we find salvation because of His atonement. In many ways we face all kinds of circumstances—joy and happiness, sadness and hatred; but in His will God knows how to accomplish His purposes. Yet there is a mystery to it all as we live through it.

The problem becomes even more compounded. All share a common destiny (v. 2). It makes no difference whether a person is righteous (a believer) or wicked, good or bad, clean or unclean. He has a sensitivity to worship God with his sacrifices or he can choose not to do so. Death awaits all. As we look about in the world today to observe all kinds of people, high and low, we recognize that in a hundred years, all present today will not be here. Death seems to have the last word. In no way do we charge the Teacher with being cynical or pessimistic. He is merely making an observation about what is all too true in this world. The proverb in the last part of verse 2 has a stark reality to it: Why should sinners and irreligious swearers be treated the same as the godly who fear God and honor and praise His name?

We protest and have every right to do so even as the Teacher did (v. 3). Is there anything other than death to which we can look forward? We feel helpless, and even indignant, as we contemplate death and our mortality. Some will conclude, therefore, that if this is all there is to life, we might just as well follow our evil and mad desires, a situation alluded to in 8:11 and 12a. But regardless of whether we give ourselves over to our evil desires, which is only madness, or become hopelessly and helplessly withdrawn, or continue to live godly and righteous lives, the end is still the same. All die.

Can we do nothing but despair? Most people seem to think not, or else all of mankind would have given up long ago in trying to find any meaning to life. The majority among the living have hope (v. 4). They cling to life because it is certainly better than nothing, which is what death appears to be. The proverb comparing the dog and the lion depicts sharply the contrast between life and death. The typical dog in the ancient Middle East was regarded as despicable as he roamed the streets, scavenging for his food; any reference to this dog brought out some of the most contemptible epithets (1 Sam. 17:43; 2 Sam. 3:8; 16:9). The lion on the other hand was regarded as the most regal among the beasts (Prov. 30:30); but once it is dead, what good is it? At least it is better to be alive, even as a contemptible dog.

Does the Teacher contradict himself? As we compare verse 4 with 4:2 and 7:1, there is a difference in perspective because in the earlier passages he had to deal with life's unhappy experiences where, from this world's viewpoint, it might be better to be rid of the pressure. In 9:4 life is viewed for the possibility of enjoyment by simply being alive. Obviously, there has to be a balance between the two extremes, sorrows and life's pleasures, which will always be a difficult riddle for people in different countries, under many different kinds of regimes, and in the midst of life's terrifying pressures.

While death comes, no one—whether believer or unbeliever—

should let this most dreadful and terrifying experience overwhelm him (vv. 5–6). Generally, to live is better than to die; and in most people there is that something that drives them on to achieve the best they can. The majority of people will be engaged in the business of making a living, having children, and hoping that the future will bring better days. There will always be those who have a drive in many pursuits of life—art, music, the production of literature, and even the concern to rectify the wrongs of the underprivileged and disadvantaged. It is wrong to take these verses out of their context and say that the Teacher is pessimistic and even contradicts what is indicated elsewhere concerning where people go after they die. Other Scriptures refer to Sheol where people are conscious in a prospectless and shadowy existence (Ps. 88:11–12) although there are expressions of hope, such as David's who was sure of dwelling in the house of the Lord forever (Ps. 23:6). The New Testament gives even further light; the rich man died and suffered in Sheol (Luke 16:23ff.); and the believer after death appears before the judgment seat of God to receive rewards, or the lack of them, for deeds in this life (2 Cor. 5:10).

But this is not the point of view of the Teacher. He does not deny the afterlife; his principle interest is in what occurs in this life. Once a person leaves this world and the vantage point of *what we know in this world*, he cannot contribute anymore to what goes on here and will receive no reward for deeds he can no longer perform. After the average person has died and a considerable time has elapsed, even the memory of him no longer remains among the people on earth. Generally, the loves, the hates, and the jealousies that were so much a part of the person who once lived in this world will be forgotten. As people in this world view it, those who have died no longer have part in any of the pursuits that go on here among men. But even knowing these things, most people still persist in their achievements while clinging to life as long as possible. Certainly the wise, the believer, will make the most of what he can do in this world because he does have to give an account (12:13–14); the New Testament proclaims the same truth, "As long as it is day, we must do the work of him who sent me. Night is coming" (John 9:4).

2. *Enjoy life while you can* (9:7–10)

The Teacher now provides some practical advice as a counterbalance to the seeming pessimism of verses 5 and 6: we can enter into the maximum of joy in spite of what is anticipated at the end of life. Live and enjoy, in spite of it all, is the encouragement offered to us.

We are told to go, that is, be about and at it concerning life, and not to keep on worrying about some of the problems that we cannot solve (v. 7). While we do not have all the answers, God does approve what we can enjoy. Food and drink are provided for our happiness and joy because this is His design for us with which we can be engaged. The white clothing, in contrast to the black robes of mourning, are for our benefit to make us joyful and happy (v. 8). The use of fragrant oil, or perfume, which is applied to the head and body, is what brings joy to the heart (Prov. 27:9); fragrant oil and happiness often appear in connection with each other (Isa. 61:3). With our Chanel perfumes today, we have no edge on the ancient world for perfumes, except that the wise advice for joy is for godly living and not for selfishness.

Love and marriage are also ours to enjoy as a gift from God (v. 9). Marriage is one of the closest bonds that affords people some of the greatest pleasures in this life. It is interesting to note that the word "enjoy" is "see" in the Hebrew text, but "enjoy" does capture a good part of the meaning of the word. The meaning describes the gamut of human emotions and pleasures to be enjoyed (Ginsburg, p. 276). What this means for marriage is that a husband and wife can enjoy each other to the fullest in emotions. This concept runs counter to the prudish one that believers are not to enjoy sexual experiences; even the New Testament stresses that the marriage bed is pure (Heb. 13:4). Obviously, illicit love is not really love at all (7:26) and leads to human wreckage and death; but God has provided a proper way to enjoy the love relationship.

The works in which we are to engage are also gifts from God and are ours to perform in accordance with the talents and gifts we have. It is a genuine blessing to be busy and working at our trade with all our might because once we leave this life we no longer can contribute to its ongoing in this world (v. 10).

A word of concern is offered at this point. As already mentioned in connection with the enjoyment of the marriage bond, there will be believers today who insist that the gifts of this life and pleasures to be enjoyed in this world are worldly and are to be shunned. Rather, say these people, it is more important to be caught up with spiritual gifts, worship of the Lord, and thinking only of spiritual blessings here and what is ahead in the presence of the Lord. But this view is a perversion of true spirituality. God ordained His gifts to be enjoyed in this life, and we can be spiritual in using this world's gifts while at the same time giving glory to God for spiritual blessings. Both Testaments emphasize a balance of earthly and spiritual gifts, and whenever either of them is pushed aside to the exclusion of the other, then we have something that is not biblical.

In conclusion, the Teacher mentions the dimension of meaningless-ness (v. 9) as a further reminder that life goes very quickly; therefore, we are not to dwell on the negative only but rather enjoy our family and work and try to be as positive as possible (v. 10). To be involved is wise advice because there is no reason to be pessimistic in this world as we understand some aspect of our part in the plan of God. Paul's advice is also comparable, "Whatever you do, work at it with all your heart, as working for the Lord, not for men" (Col. 3:23). As indicated in the Introduction, this activity keeps God in the center of everything we do as we live and work in this world.

The phrase of going to the "grave" (Sheol, v. 10) will lead some to say that the Teacher has no concept of life after this life. But is it fair to the Teacher that because he treats the subject of how we are to live here and now, we therefore conclude that the wise man denies immortality, or claims that there is no life to enjoy beyond this world? Let us not build on an argument from silence that because a writer does not mention all there is to say on a subject, he therefore does not believe it. The wise man does talk about our having to face God when He will examine all our deeds (12:14). Does this sound like he has no concept of afterlife? We need to simply let the Teacher say what he has to say about this life and not read into the text what is not there.

I. Time and Chance but Recognize a Higher Power (9:11–12)

Once again the Teacher returns to the baffling themes of life. Even as he had to say, with a heavy heart, that righteous men receive what the wicked deserve while the wicked enjoy the blessings of the right-eous (8:14), so likewise we recognize another seeming injustice when success does not always come to those who merit it the most (v. 11). Again it is a situation where we do not have all the facts of life or the total plan as God sees it, which might explain why the "most deserv-ing" do not receive their just reward.

Events can occur that change our modes of living in a moment's time. Those who are the swiftest runners do not always reach their goals; some disease may cripple them and then their running days are over. The strongest do not necessarily win all the battles; presidents and other rulers can be assassinated in the prime of life. Whatever the baffling reasons, there is no guarantee that the wise will even be able to earn a living, that the most brilliant will be able to amass wealth, or that the learned men of ability will have influence or reputation. Instead, the Teacher concludes that time and "chance" seemingly play a part in life's pursuits. Life is paradoxical; and while we work with all of our might to gain what brings us happiness and joy, nevertheless success and favor (or the means to make a living) are not ours to control. Contrary to an optimistic humanism that declares that man is the master of his own fate and captain of his own ship, we have to learn there are purposes of God beyond our comprehension.

The word "chance" may be an unfortunate translation because it may convey the idea that there is no rhyme nor reason as to why life's events happen. The Hebrew word *(pega')* means accident, adversity, or disappointment. For example, Solomon said, as he combined this word with "evil," that no disaster, or evil occurrence, had befallen him as he entered into his kingship (1 Kings 5:4; verse 18 in the Hebrew text). The point, therefore, is that in the counsels of God things happen over which we have no control, but wisdom teaches us that we have to recognize that He knows what He is doing. Unsaved man may believe that "chance" explains unforeseen events, but the believer should know better.

The Teacher adds that no person can know when his or her hour will come (v. 12). This verse might have the idea of the end of life, but it could also refer to what was discussed in the preceding verse. As man is involved with the pursuits of life, he does not know when the hour of his "time and accident" or misfortune will come to him. Even as the fishermen cast their nets for the unsuspecting fish and as birds suddenly are caught in the snare, so we can be caught at an evil time. These times break in so suddenly on us that we are unable to prepare for such an occurrence. Once again we are reminded that whether in the daily experiences of life or when our lives come to an end we cannot control entirely the events in which we find ourselves. King Ahab had every reason to believe that he could capture Ramoth Gilead from the Syrians; the arrow that took his life in the heat of battle came at random, at a time when Ahab was not expecting it (2 Chron. 18:33). In his case, however, he was forewarned and he will never be able to

deny it (2 Chron. 18:19). The prophet Micaiah had pulled back the
curtains on some of God's purposes and revealed to Ahab what was
going to befall him. The Teacher here is only trying to tell us that from
this world's point of view, we can enjoy many facets of this life (9:7–10);
but there is a higher Power who works in our lives. Certainly we
believers, even though we do not have all of God's purposes revealed
to us, can be testimonies to the people of this world that often God tries
to speak to us through the "times and chances" so people might listen
to the wisdom that comes from Him and thereby turn to Him.

J. Wisdom Versus Wealth and Power (9:13–18)

The Teacher provides us with a statement that wisdom apart from
wealth and power can be unappreciated. Many attempts have been
made to find some historical incident for the lesson that the Teacher
derives, concerning the deliverance of the city through the interven-
tion of a wise person and his advice, such as the deliverance of Abel
Beth Maacah by a certain wise woman (2 Sam. 20:15ff.). But not even
her name has been preserved, and this might give rise to the fact that
once her services were over her wisdom was unappreciated. Most
likely, however, the Teacher gave us a typical case in order to demonstrate wisdom versus wealth and power.

He tells a tale concerning a small city with only a few people in it (vv.
14–15). A powerful and great king laid seige to the city, and its surren-
der and destruction seemed almost imminent. It has all too often been
the case in both the ancient and modern worlds that conquering armies
have ravaged their enemies, breaking down the defenses of a city and
slaughtering its inhabitants. In the frantic defense by the city's inhabitants, a poor but wise man was able to more than match wits with the
great and powerful invader, and the city was spared. But once the
victory was won, the poor wise man faded again into the background
from where he came and succeeding generations no longer remembered him. Not even a monument or a word in the history books gave
him his due as a memorial. This is too often a sad but true account.

The conclusion obviously has to recognize the fact that wisdom has
the means to save and to spare not only a city, but also an individual
from life's problems that assault him from every side (vv. 16–18). The
wise man was poverty-stricken; but as soon as he gave his services and
the problems were solved, he was of no real consequence to the
wealthy and powerful leaders and people. The tragedy is that only an

outward respect was accorded to the wise man, and he was not appreciated for what he really was.

Outwardly the words of the wise calmly heard in quiet are of more value and are greater than the cry of a ruler among fools (v. 17). Perhaps the great king, while attacking the city, was regarded as a noisy person shouting lustily along with the soldiers attempting to break into the city. But when the good people of the city no longer needed the poor wise man, it appears that they were no better off than the fools on the outside trying to break in.

The conclusion is that wisdom is better than all the weapons of war, better than the huge sums of money required to produce the weapons, and better still than the warriors who handle the armaments (v. 18). The Teacher is speaking only in general truths to say that wise people are always forgotten. Most of the time, however, they are; but one rich and powerful sinner can have a far-reaching influence that destroys much good wrought through wisdom. This fact is one of those wrenching experiences of life as a particular truth. On the other hand, as already pointed out, God-fearing and wise men will in the *long run* be better off than evil people with their momentary schemes (8:12).

K. Facing Life's Peculiar Situations (10:1–20)

The Teacher takes up a variety of situations that treat a number of facets of life. By means of proverbs we are encouraged to live according to a moral standard that can fit the many dimensions of life. By means of pithy sayings, taunt, and tease, we are encouraged to follow the wise teaching of wisdom that will help us to avoid the pitfalls of life.

1. *How the fool loses his way* (10:1–3)

How many times have we seen it to be true that it takes only one person to create enough havoc to overcome the good of many? The Teacher vividly demonstrates this theme.

Dead flies, or flies of death, can also be understood as flies about to die (v. 1). As these insects struggle and then fall into and float on the surface of the mixture of oil and perfume, their corrupting bodies make the perfume bubble or ferment; what was supposed to be sweet smelling becomes a foul odor.

The comparison now becomes quite apt. One dying fly can ruin expensive perfume. By comparison, a little folly also corrupts, but how little is needed? It is the smallest amount, even one act, that can weigh more than wisdom and honor! It is indeed a sobering thought. One reckless instance can forfeit the attainment of a goal or mar a good beginning. Illustrations abound in Scripture. Esau was reckless, and a little of the lentil stew was his undoing from which he never recovered. Even wise people can act foolishly. David's one look at Bathsheba brought him a lot of grief.

The discourse continues on the nature and acts of a fool (vv. 2–3). The reference to the heart's inclination toward right or left appears to be a practical connotation that can lead to a moral one. Widespread belief of ancient days regarded the right hand as more skilled to do life's tasks while the left appeared to be more awkward. This is only a general truth because there were sons of Benjamin who were left-handed and yet could sling stones at a hair and not miss (Judg. 20:16). The moral, however, is built on the commonly accepted way in which the two hands are used. The heart of a wise man inclines toward the right; such a person enjoys advantages and aids in his pursuits. On the other hand, the fool, as he inclines toward the left, finds himself in disastrous circumstances. In the moral sense, he does that which is opposite to the wise person.

The thought is continued in verse 3. Even as the fool walks along the road, his heart or understanding fails him; as he moves about in public, it is apparent that his sense is not there at all. He demonstrates that he is stupid and everyone knows it. The Book of Proverbs dwells considerably on the heartset of the fool: 1) If he would only keep silent, he might appear to be wise (Prov. 17:28); but unfortunately he does not have the intelligence to keep quiet; 2) his lips and the words from his mouth bring him only disaster (Prov. 18:6); 3) he does not even take the trouble to listen and learn (Prov. 18:2); 4) when a message is sent with the fool, he never gets it right (Prov. 26:6); 5) when a fool tries to speak wisdom, it is painful to listen to (Prov. 26:9). The fool has many ways of revealing himself; and while it may be the plot of a comedy play, yet it is tempered by tragedy for the person who brings only disaster on himself.

2. *The politics of upside down* (10:4–7)

The Teacher turns to another topic to consider the erratic circumstances of politics. Working with government leaders and bureaucratic officials can be unnerving at times; these leaders are human as they give vent to their anger and nasty tempers when anyone asks a favor of them. The word "anger" in Hebrew is "spirit" and can also mean resentment or temper (Judg. 8:3; Prov. 29:11). When the anger of a leader or official rises against his servant or employee, the latter is advised not to get his "huff" (anger) up and leave his post (v. 4). The warning previously had been issued about people leaving their posts (8:3), but the advice can bear repetition. People often become impatient, demand their own way, and resign positions because of a false pride. These reactions reflect immaturity. At other times, there may be reason to react, but matters of personal relationships should not be solved in angry action and reaction. Rather, calmness or composure allay or lay to rest great errors or offenses (Prov. 16:14; 12:18). For both the ruler or government official or the employee in his insubordination, it is good advice for people who like to "blow their stacks" and then repent at leisure for their wrongdoing!

The Teacher has no illusions about people, even rulers and officials in high places (10:5–7). One thing we learn with certainty is that we do not live in a society of permanence; events happen so quickly that we are amazed and wonder how they all took place. The wise man pondered many such situations that take place in government leadership and pronounced them as an evil, namely, the error or unwitting sin of a ruler (v. 5). The consequences of his deplorable decisions (3:16; 4:1ff.; 5:8) are such that he is swept out of office through resignation or revolution. But those who follow are often no better than their predecessors; successors can be downright fools (v. 6)! The picture of contrast describes the disgusting situation: Fools are in high positions while slaves ride proudly on horseback as if they are valiant conquerors (v. 7; cf. Prov. 19:10). The rich and the princes who are degraded are no doubt those who were trained and prepared to be leaders in government. But they did not prove wise in their leadership and ruled only to suit themselves. These situations happen all too frequently; and because of wrong decisions, intrigue, bribes, etc., which occur in government affairs, people then have to suffer the consequences.

"Why should it happen?" many have cried. But once again we have difficulty discerning the entire plan of God. Revolution can get rid of one set of problems with officials, but another set will come along. Or God can permit these circumstances to bring a people to Himself, such as many of the tribes in ancient Israel during the period of the judges. For whatever reason, however, we have to trust God and realize that

His wisdom is beyond ours. For our part, we make as much of life as we can in the midst of disastrous political and economic consequences.

3. Use your common sense (10:8–11)

In addition to the higher and most complex problems of life, we still must use the common sense of wisdom to be careful in everything we do. A number of proverbs abound in general rules that will help us for our usual everyday needs.

People who dig pits may fall into them (vv. 8–9). Whoever breaks through walls, perhaps to build larger enclosures, may be bitten by snakes who nestle in the crevices of the walls. Those who quarry stones may be injured by the effort in extracting them; sometimes these are huge blocks of stone that are required in large buildings. In splitting logs, pieces of wood may strike a person in his vulnerable places, such as the eyes. Consequently, a person who uses his common sense will take measures to protect himself. It is only the fool who does not consider the dangers involved in these tasks and can therefore injure himself permanently and no longer be able to work.

Many have been the attempts to derive "deeper" truths concerning the dull ax and the skill of its use when it is sharpened (v. 10): 1) "Wisdom is more powerful than iron weapons" (Rashi); 2) "Wisdom is better than labor" (Ibn Ezra); 3) "In resisting tyranny with inadequate means, the rebel succeeds only in strengthening the army of the tyrant" (Ginsburg) (Gordis, pp. 321, 322). It is best, however, to continue with the parallel in the context and consider it another piece of wise advice. For a person to work with an ax, that is, the metal part, when it is dull and its edge is unsharpened, he has to exert more strength to accomplish his task. Why be lazy and work harder than is necessary? The idea is to take the time and know beforehand what is necessary to do the job correctly. If a person wants to have a proper instrument with which to work, then he will sharpen the ax, thereby doing more and better work and profiting in the long run. The Teacher is taunting the workman; the advice should be taken well so he will be successful.

There seems to be a touch of sarcasm concerning the snake charmer (literally, master of the tongue) when he has not properly charmed the snake for whatever tricks are to be performed (v. 11). If the charmer has not taken the necessary time to accomplish his task and is bitten by the snake, then there can be no advantage (yitron; cf. 1:3; 2:13; 5:15) in his business. In this case, with no advantage, there is no fee; and the charmer has lost out because he has not used his common sense to properly prepare for his means of livelihood.

4. *Wise people and fools* (10:12–15)

The Teacher takes up the theme again on why it is better to be wise than be a fool and that wisdom is better than folly. Proverbs therefore are provided for helpful application in what should be regarded as the everyday arena of life. In no way should an exegete look for a multiplicity of hidden meanings that do violence to the text.

The use of words in wisdom are of paramount importance. In the interaction of personal relationships in everyday life, the wise man knows how to be gracious, that is, his mouth frames words of grace (v. 12). They win for him favor because the words come from an understanding heart (Prov. 13:15) and even the king or leading authorities will be his friend (Prov. 22:11). The point is that when a person has learned how to fear the Lord, he will be on the road to learning true wisdom; and his mouth and speech will reflect it.

The fool is the exact opposite. The comedy-tragedy of the fool was already pictured in 10:3, but now the Teacher continues with this theme.

The fool talks too much (v. 14), which means that before his brain can even think and then gear itself to his mouth, the mouth is moving and he does not even consider what he is saying. Out come the words and everyone around him knows him for what he is. From the beginning, his words are foolishness or absurdity; in the end, after the process has come to its dreadful conclusion, the words that proceed from his mouth have taken on a wicked madness (v. 13). While the wise man is characterized as one who fears the Lord, the fool (thick-brained) is the one who despises wisdom and discipline (Prov. 1:7b). His madness reflects his mental and moral wickedness because he does not fear the Lord. It is sheer madness to turn away from a reverence toward God and the wisdom that leads a person to live godly before Him. In the end the words that come from the lips of a fool will destroy him (literally, swallow him up).

The familiar theme that no one knows what is coming (cf. 8:7) is seen in connection with the fool's talk (v. 14). Since he talks before he even thinks, how is he to be aware of the future in his ignorance? At least the wise man ponders the mystery that the future holds for him, but the fool has not learned to keep quiet and learn a deep truth. Jesus likewise called a farmer a fool when he could only prattle about how many barns he would have to build to contain his goods (Luke 12:18–20). The difference, however, between the Teacher and Jesus is that the former talked in terms of what will happen in the future of this life while Jesus extended the view into what happens after this life.

But even more tragic is the fool who talks so much that he actually tires himself out (v. 15). He has not learned anything because he has been continually talking; and as a result, he cannot even do the simplest of things. The Teacher proclaims what must have been a general proverb, "He (the fool) does not know the way to town." We have a similar saying today of the senseless person: "He doesn't know enough to come in out of the rain!" All a fool does is talk and babble; consequently, he never learns about the wisdom of God, the problems of life, the plan of God that is difficult enough to understand on our part, and how we should live in the give and take of relationships. There is a touch of mockery with the attempt to make the fool realize his tragic mistake in that he has made life more difficult for himself by his obstinacy. It is important in everyday life to learn to be quiet and listen to the wisdom from God lest we end up making fools of ourselves.

5. Wisdom and kings and rulers (10:16–20)

Proverbs for everyday life are applicable to rulers too. After all, they must have wisdom that will help them rule wisely, dispense justice, and make proper use of their time in their ministry. The Teacher had described the wrong decisions made by a ruler and their consequences in 10:4–7, but now he returns to the theme to give his advice on how to avoid wicked, foolish decisions.

The word "woe" (translated "pity" in 4:10) is here directed to the land and its inhabitants (v. 16). How unfortunate it is for the people of a country as well as for the production of the economy when the king or leader is a child! This incongruous picture was given in verses 6 and 7 where servants ride as leaders while the princes walk as the servants had formerly done. The word for "child" is the Hebrew na'ar and generally refers to a young person, either in the teen years or in early manhood. (Or, as in the NIV, the government of the country has been taken over by one who was once a young servant to the king.)

Whether lad or servant, the reins of government are in the hands of the immature and inexperienced while those capable of ruling, the

princes, are feasting in the morning, eating for eating's sake. It is not
wrong to have breakfast, but for leaders to linger long at the table and
eat and eat is an abuse of rulership. This does not refer only to eating;
drinking also is included. We see the officials begin their feasting and
drinking in the morning and continue all day long (Isa. 5:11, 22). What
happens to the affairs of state that should be in the hands of the wisest
and most sober people for the best political and economic management
of a nation?

No wonder the Teacher cried out with an exclamation of anguish for
the people of a country caught in such a trap. The end result can only
mean either the downfall of a country and an easy prey for invading
conquerors or a revolution to change this situation whereby the common people are able to enter into the fruits of their labors. It is a
pointed lesson to leaders and rulers that they have a responsibility to
rule wisely and carry forward every level of government with prudence.

On the other hand, there is a commendation for wise kings and
princes (v. 17). O the happiness, or joy, of a land whose worthy king,
according to the Teacher, is one born and bred to his position and not a
slave or child who has become a king whom people cannot bear (Prov.
30:21–22). The emphasis is not on snobbishness but rather on the
upper class and particularly those people who were taught by wise men
to have a true understanding of wisdom and human nature. Wisdom
insists that princes as leaders eat at the proper time and only what is
necessary to have strength for their tasks. Gluttony and drunkenness
are one major downfall of a nation, particularly as leaders wile away
the time to serve only themselves.

It might appear that the proverbs of verses 18 and 19 have little to do
with the two preceding verses. Some suggest the house to be a figure
for the state (Leupold, p. 251); as a house can fall into disrepair, so the
state can be disreputable with irresponsible leaders. But we need not
allegorize the exegesis. It is best to understand the verse as an analogy
that if people abandon their responsibilities for the upkeep of their
houses, they will fall into disrepair. But in the same way, if nobles and
leaders are going to eat and drink all day long, thereby abandoning the
affairs of state, the country will go into ruination. One does not have to
do anything to cause a house to decay, rot, and eventually fall down;
similarly, when leaders are lazy and find it difficult to lift their hands to
exercise their responsibilities, a government and country will suffer

drastically. Laziness is one form of foolishness and reveals a sad lack of wisdom.

The meaning of a feast made for laughter and wine that makes for a merry life (v. 19) is left in such a way that it could refer back to either the princes who have nothing to do but eat and drink all day or to those leaders who eat at the proper time and do not drink to become drunk. The use of wine in the Old Testament is with approbation; wine gladdens the heart of man (Ps. 104:15), and wine is a symbol of joy. Therefore, wicked kings and princes can turn their banquet tables into revelry and think of nothing else all day long. With this example, ordinary people likewise become idle and lazy. On the other hand, there is a proper time and place for man to eat his bread with gladness and drink the wine with which God cheers the heart so that kings can rule with wisdom and citizens can work with a sense of blessing. Literally, the last line of the verse simply says, "money answers to all." Money is what makes possible a person's pursuits in life, either for evil or good. Whatever a person wants to make of it, he uses it accordingly, thereby providing the clue that verse 19 is a general truth—for good or evil.

Finally, after discussing kings and rulers as they ought to be and unfortunately when many times they are not, the Teacher now suggests again (8:2ff.) that a person must not revile the king even in the inner region of his thoughts (v. 20). Neither should he revile the rich in his bedroom. There is a parallelism between the king and the rich because those with wealth generally were in the ruling class. Perhaps there is reason for questioning stupid decisions of rulers who bring disaster on a nation, but there is the call for prudence and the proper time to correct such decisions (cf. 8:6ff.). Caution and prudence dictate that a person should think twice before starting gossip about how terrible kings and rulers are in their decisions. Perhaps this loose talk is a hint at insurrection. In the ancient world, as it is too often true today, rumors and disgruntled talk could be carried far and wide. Statements uttered in private in the morning made the rounds of the town and met the teller again in the evening where he least expected to encounter them. The proverb concerning the birds that carry gossip and rumors sounds like modern proverbs, such as "Even the walls have ears"! The sophisticated use of electronics in our day to listen to conversation is not that much improvement over the ancient world; rulers then did a good job of eavesdropping and knew quite well what was going on among the population so as to control any rebels and disgruntled people.

L. On Being Diligent (11:1–6)

The proverbial sayings in chapter 10 help a person to observe, examine, and guide in the most fundamental concerns of life in chapter 11.

Two different interpretations appear in the commentaries regarding bread cast on the waters (v. 1). One view says the exhortation is to be generous to fellow human beings. On first glance it might seem that as we cast our bread on the waters in generosity, it will come back to us in even greater spiritual and material blessings. An example of an ancient sense is, "Scatter thy bread on the water and on the dry land; in the end of the days thou findest it again" (Ben Sira, an Aramaic proverb, cited by Delitzsch, p. 391). There is also the story of the one who threw the Eastern kind of bread, thin round cakes, into the river and these easily floated; hungry people downstream were able to fish the cakes out of the water and thereby have food for themselves (Delitzsch, pp. 391, 392). Some modern interpreters follow the same understanding that the wise person should practice charity in sharing with others who are less fortunate (Leupold, p. 255). The point of verse 2 also suggests charitable interests since there may come the time when a person is not able to give (Acts 11:27–30).

There is another, more appropriate view of the Teacher's emphasis. He is talking about sending a person's bread, that is, his substance, on the surface of the water through ships to carry on a trade with foreign countries (Ps. 107:23, where there were merchants on the mighty waters). Delitzsch (p. 392), Gordis (p. 330), and other modern interpreters take this view. We shall make reference to both views as we proceed in this section.

It would not be strange in Solomon's day to trade by means of the fleet that sailed from the port of Ezion Geber, which was not too far from the present Eilat on the shores of the Red Sea (1 Kings 9:26). The ships sailed to Ophir, trading Israel's products for gold. Reference is made also to the king's fleet of trading ships of Tarshish along with the ships of Tyre which went on commercial ventures every three years, returning with gold, silver, ivory, apes, and baboons (1 Kings 10:22). This type of commercial adventure would not be entirely unknown to the Teacher, and his advice therefore was to be diligent with the means at hand in order to profit from our labors. The point is not to be greedy so as to have no thought for anything or anyone else; wisdom had instructed us that the pursuit of material possessions in themselves is meaningless (2:4ff.).

The phrase about giving portions to seven or eight (v. 2) refers to investments in a commercial adventure that should be divided in seven or eight ways. This idea of division is seen also in how Joshua apportioned land to the tribes (Josh. 18:5). We have seen proverbs where the wisdom writer uses numbers, not in a literal sense but in a general way of speaking by suggesting a number, although he could go on to mention even more; for example, the three and four (Prov. 30:15ff.) and the six and seven (Prov. 6:16ff.) are ways of saying that even more could be mentioned. The Teacher advises that in commercial adventures a person should not put every bit of money into one basket. Who knows if a disaster will destroy everything since the future cannot be predicted with any certainty. Rather a person is to divide investments into seven, eight, or more ventures so that he will be assured of as much a return as possible. The art of practicing business requires common sense, and the Teacher has a lot of experience in acquiring material possessions.

A lesson on diligence with our investments also is provided in verses 3 and 4. With the right atmospheric conditions when rain clouds are full of moisture, rain will fall on the earth; and the prevailing winds that come as a result will cause trees to sway. Some trees will be blown down, falling either toward the south or the north depending on which way the wind blows. These are familiar phenomena of nature. The point is now made: Do not spend too much needless time watching to see whether it is going to rain or whether there is going to be a hurricane, but "on with your work!" (Gordis, p. 331). Man cannot bend the forces of nature to his own liking because they follow their own laws, and we know only too well that disasters can come (v. 2). At the same time, we are encouraged to be diligent in every new venture and not paralyze ourselves with the qualms of what might go wrong.

Another example is provided whereby we have to continue with our work in spite of uncertainty (v. 5). Reference was made concerning the inability to control the wind (8:8); that idea is emphasized again. Today modern meteorology attempts to plot the path of storms and winds, yet even with the most advanced information we still must confess a wide area of ignorance in predicting with certainty the course of the wind, to say nothing about the inability to control it. Man also has to confess the lack of knowledge as to how a body is formed in a mother's womb, a mystery expressed in other parts of the Old Testament (Ps. 139:13–16;

Job 10:11–12). Today we may be on the threshold of knowledge in this area; but even with our most modern equipment, the research is still in its most elementary stages. These are only two illustrations to remind us that the totality of the work of God the Maker is still very much a mystery, a theme that the Teacher has mentioned a number of times. Once again the point is that man should not spend a lot of useless time trying to get at ultimate knowledge, the essence of wisdom, in order to be able to predict all events. To spend too much time in this search will paralyze man in his diligence *to do* what he is able.

Mere idle speculation is a luxury in which only a few can be engaged. Most people in the work-a-day world have to be diligent, sow seed (start to work) early in the morning (v. 6), be industrious the rest of the day, and not be idle in the evening hours. Life has enough of its mysteries and difficulties, but we are encouraged to do what we can and not speculate about which venture will be good and which one will fail. Diligence will have its reward in its due time even though some of the fruits may be lost. It is a precious lesson to learn, first of all, not to pursue any one interest to the exclusion of others and second, to always be involved with as much as possible. The work ethic of wisdom is repeated in the New Testament whereby we are to make the most of everything possible in all seasons (Eph. 5:16; 2 Tim. 4:2ff.).

When we interpret this passage as a lesson on benevolence, we are encouraged to practice kindness and interest in the needs of those less fortunate. Such a practice will have its reward in due time, not as a selfish motive but in the sense that God does repay in many ways those interested in alleviating human misery and suffering. With this view we are encouraged to be as generous as is possible with as many people as we can with the means available. Life's problems will come, but we cannot spend our time trying to figure them out or finding the most opportune time for our benevolence. Even as the farmer must be diligent, in spite of the weather, we have to be interested continually in others and help them as much as possible.

M. A Word to the Young (11:7–12:8)

The Teacher returns to consider the ever-recurring theme that the blessings and gifts of life are ours to enjoy as we take and use them. Time soon will come when the body will be ravaged and these gifts will no longer be pleasurable.

1. *Enjoy!* (11:7–10)

The wise Teacher captures for us some of the many facets of life—the joys to be experienced as well as the days of darkness (vv. 7–8). Life has its many patterns, and included in the picture are those experiences with which we take pleasure and those that turn us off. The ability to enjoy life is pictured in terms of everyday experiences. Light is sweet, and it is pleasant to see the rays of sunlight. Who has not taken pleasure in the radiance of light on a warm spring morning after the dull gray of winter? But this is only a small measure of all that the Teacher told us to enjoy all the days of our lives (9:7–10). There is no need to become morbid, thinking about death all the time (although it was mentioned that both the factors of life and death are what makes one appreciate life with its perspectives, 7:1ff.). So as long as possible and with a hopeful, optimistic mood, we are to enjoy the delights that are ours to experience because the days of darkness eventually will come. By no means is the Teacher an Epicurean where all he can think of is "Eat, drink, and be merry, for tomorrow we die." There is no moral in this mindset; rather, wisdom insists that there is a moral of God that we must realize in the midst of the pursuits of life's delights as well as the dread prospects of the sorrows of this world.

The days of darkness may not necessarily refer to the day of death, although it is a likely possibility; rather, the description refers mainly to the losses, sufferings, and tragedies of life, the counterbalances to joy. These frustrating experiences can be meaningless from this world's understanding and knowledge, but many times these wrongs are what makes the joys all the more precious.

The theme of enjoying life is continued (vv. 9–10). The young person particularly is encouraged to be happy, to let his heart give him joy, and to follow the ways of his heart and whatever his eyes can see. This advice becomes a healthy counterbalance to those moralists who seem to feel that there is nothing in this life to enjoy. Three times the Teacher expressed this aspect of enjoying life as an imperative, 11:7–8a, b; 11:9; 11:10a, b (Gordis, p. 336). This joy is tempered by the facts that the young person should remember the coming days of darkness and that everything to come appears to be meaningless or fleeting at best. Even youth and vigor (*shaharuth*, translated occasionally as "times of black hair" in the Jewish sources, Delitzsch, p. 401) are only temporal; the time will come when it will be difficult to enjoy life, as we shall see in 12:2ff.

The Teacher assigns another reason for balance while enjoying life: God must be kept in the center of all pursuits of life and its enjoyment because there will be a day of judgment. This statement anticipated the final conclusion of the book, but already there is a warning not to pervert the joys of this life, become Epicurean, descend into the reprehensible practice of immorality, and pervert the riches of this world to become self-centered. The encouragement to enjoy in moderation and within the moral bounds set forth by God echoes Moses' instruction that a person must not prostitute himself "by going after the lusts of your own hearts and eyes" (Num. 15:39). It is a hard lesson to learn, even for godly believers, that God has given us joys in this life that we should not shun nor feel that they are "worldly." Remember the balance while we enjoy!

2. *Remember the admonition while young* (12:1)

The Teacher graphically sets forth what follows youth and vigor (or the time of the black hair). Before a person comes to old age and makes the judgment that youth and the prime of life are fleeting, he is instructed to remember the Creator in the days of his youth. We are admonished to lay it to heart before we pervert the joys of this world that there is an ultimate purpose to life even though it may not be fully ascertained in this world. God has implanted in our hearts the appreciation for eternity (3:11), but we can mess up His intentions and wishes (7:29) and might have a tendency to make any one area of life our total interest. We are encouraged, therefore, to commit ourselves to our Creator while we have our wits about us, while we can still enjoy life, and before we lose the fullest capacity to even think of God's purposes and desires. We prepare our hearts for these ultimate issues while we are young, before time slips away from our grasp. The days of trouble, the failure of bodily and mental strength, and the lack of pleasure in any pursuits of life are not the occasions to begin to think of a godly lifestyle in this world and of an ultimate accountability to God.

It is interesting that the word "Creator" is plural which some say suggests the mystery of plurality of the Godhead. But it is wrong to read back into the Old Testament, particularly into the world view of the Teacher, this fuller revelation of the New Testament. It is best to regard the plural of "Creator" as an emphasis on His majesty since the Hebrew plural in one respect accentuates quality or quantity in the superlative sense.

3. *How we grow old* (12:2-8)

A number of possibilities are provided by different interpreters to describe the imagery the Teacher used concerning the onset of old age. (See Gordis, pp. 338–339, for six views!) Two views in particular are the most likely ways to understand the poetic imagery: 1) The loss of vitality in old age is likened to the disrepair of a wealthy estate. The guardians at the gates grow old and feeble, the slave women who grind away at the mill become few, the aging women of the house no longer look out through the windows (vv. 3–4), and the wells are inoperable (v. 6). While this interpretation fits verses 3, 4, and 6, it is difficult to apply this explanation for verses 2, 5, and 7 which do not relate to the old estate. 2) A better interpretation is to accept the first view of a decaying mansion as allegory for verses 3, 4, and 6 but also to use a general metaphor or literal interpretation for the other verses, all of which depict the aging of the body.

We begin to see the impending debility of old age in verse 2, which refers to the natural phenomena of heavenly bodies and clouds. Sun and light are experiences to be enjoyed (11:7); but darkness is associated with what is unpleasant and, even worse, with judgment and punishment (Joel 2:10; Amos 8:9; Ezek. 32:7). At times clouds are also descriptions of punishment (Ezek. 13:11–13; 38:22). The Teacher, however, draws on the natural phenomena of the lengthening shadows of evening, the waning of moon and stars, as well as the clouds reforming and becoming dark and menacing again after a torrential downfall of rain. The description is an imagery of impending darkness when, applied to the onset of old age, joys and happiness are less and less of a pleasure. Difficult as it may be to contemplate such an experience, yet it is nevertheless a fact of life; as a person gets older his faculties, mental and physical strength, and the use of the body organs diminish. Hence, the admonition to remember to honor the Lord and acquire wisdom for a godly lifestyle before these experiences come upon us. It is questionable to seek any deeper meanings in verse 2 where the sun is equated with the spirit of man, light represents his clear thought, the moon represents the soul, and the stars are the five senses (Delitzsch, p. 404) because there is a problem trying to establish these allegorical assertions based on a more literal interpretation of the text.

This talk about old age and the waning of our faculties might be too gloomy to contemplate, but the Teacher wants to emphasize the point that it is always best to make decisions for the Lord when a person is young. If he has to go into the details of how pathetic man becomes in his older years to prove his point, he will do it to convince youth to listen to reason. He begins by mentioning the debilitating symptoms of the various parts of the body and picturing the increasing difficulty an elderly person has in his everyday functioning.

While verse 2 was more of an analogy, we now note the allegory of the estate fallen into disrepair when only a few are left to manage its upkeep (v. 3). The keepers of the house are generally those servants involved in the everyday operation. In application, these refer to the hands and arms as well as possibly the sides of the body or ribs. The strong men of the house are those appointed to guard it; as they stoop, they picture the aged legs that become bent and the knees that shake. The grinders (Heb., feminine) refer to the women who used to grind out the grain for the daily supply of flour for baking; as they age, there were only a few to do the work. The phrase is an apt description of teeth that become few in old age, and those that remain can no longer chew food. Those who look out the window (Heb., feminine) refer to the aged women of the house who were no longer able to mingle in public and therefore gazed through the lattice windows to observe what was going on, even as Michal looked out the window (2 Sam. 6:16). This phrase speaks of the eyes that become dim, possibly because of cataracts or other eye diseases of old age.

The allegory continues to describe the decaying estate (v. 4) and its application. Homes in the Middle East were enclosed by walls, the front wall facing the street, usually abutting it. The gate at the street opened into a courtyard, and the house was located at the rear of the enclosure. The closing of the doors at the street picture the closing down of the apertures of the body, that is, either the mouth or the ears. In the case of the mouth, because of so few teeth, the lips and cheeks sag into the mouth. It is interesting that Job referred to the leviathan (possibly crocodile) whose doors of the mouth no one dared open (Job 41:14). On the other hand, because of the second line of the verse that refers to the difficulty of hearing, doors could refer to the ears; as one becomes older, it is more and more difficult to hear properly. The fading of the sound of grinding, perhaps a reference to the few women who ground out the grain, is the description of the fading of one's ability to hear.

The last two lines of verse 4 are to be taken more literally, rather than as an allegory referring to the old estate. Men who rise up at the sound of birds can refer to the older person who sleeps lightly and is awakened by the singing of the birds in the morning. It might even be the description of the person who is startled by the early morning bird songs. The songs that grow faint (literally, "all the daughters of song will be brought low") could refer to the diminishing capability of the older person to hear the sound of the birds. On the other hand, the description of the daughters of song can mean "songs, melodious notes" (BDB, p. 123), which then pictures how the elderly person can no longer hear and appreciate, or finds it difficult to take the time to enjoy the musical efforts of musicians.

In another literal description of the elderly, they become terrified of any height, and one of their chief fears is that they will fall (v. 5); stairs or the slope of a hill are difficult to maneuver. Being on the street with traffic, encountering barking dogs, or disliking others to see him as he is all contribute to his fear of danger on the streets. The first tree to bloom in the land of Israel, even before winter is over, is the almond tree with its white blossoms, an apt representation of the head of white hair. The grasshopper that drags itself along is the pathetic description of the halting gait of the elderly who may have to use canes or walkers to move about because of limbs that have become crippled, perhaps due to arthritis. Desires are no longer stirred, perhaps a reference to the sexual drive and power. Some versions following the Septuagint translate "desire" as "caperberry", a kind of berry used as a stimulant for the appetite. Thus the older person no longer can appreciate this stimulus because of the failure of his physical appetites and desires.

The last two lines of verse 5 are very straightforward. The eternal home refers to the death of the older person. Jewish people use this phrase to designate the cemetery, *bet 'olam,* house of eternity or eternal home. As the body was carried to the grave professional mourners were hired to precede the column as it wended its way to the cemetery (Jer. 9:17ff.).

Verse 6 begins with an indefinite reference, "before the silver cord is severed"; therefore, the admonition "remember him" is added although it is not in the Hebrew text. Certainly there is a plaintive reminder, after describing some of the characteristics of old age, that one remember this picture while he is young. Some day he will be old too. It seems that the first two lines are an allegory of dissolution, highly figurative language of the fragility of life.

So many interpretations have been provided for the meaning of the silver cord (spine), the golden bowl (skull or brain), the pitcher (stomach or heart), and the wheel (body or circulatory system). (See Gordis, p. 348.) Since commentators do not agree on the meaning of the various figures, it is best not to speculate but rather to see a reference to literal figures that then depict the death of the aged person. Since this verse follows through from the last two lines of verse 5, it is safe to assume that the Teacher continues his very graphic description of how life can end.

The wise man could have referred to an actual situation whereby a silver cord, to which some object had been attached, was anchored to and suspended from a ceiling. When the cord was severed, having become frayed, the object that was attached fell to the floor and broke. The golden bowl can be an allusion to that which contained the oil that fed the flame in the lamp of the seven-branched candlestick in the Temple (Zech. 4:2), but probably the Teacher was referring to a single lamp hammered out of a piece of gold that was suspended by a cord from the ceiling of a palatial home or temple. At any rate, something happened, the cord was severed, and the bowl was dropped so that it smashed. Without pushing the figures too far, the implication is clear: Life is fragile and ends, even as the silver cord is severed and the golden bowl is broken. Perhaps the use of the figures of gold and silver mean that life is precious but will end some day.

Furthermore, the figure of the pitcher shattered at the spring or well and the broken wheel return us to the figure of the dilapidated mansion. The clay pitcher once used to draw water from the spring or well lies smashed in many pieces of potsherds. The wheel that enabled the rope to be let down for water is broken and unusable for the purpose it was designed. The sight of the shattered pitcher and broken wheel can also picture the fragility of life; with age likewise the body breaks down and eventually dies.

After death, the dust from the body that disintegrated returns to the ground from where it came (v. 7), a reference to what the Teacher declared in 3:20 and a reminder of Genesis 3:19. The spirit returns to God who gave it, described in 3:21. The object of the wise man is not to develop a fully grown wisdom doctrine concerning the afterlife but rather to consider the real possibility that the spirit is indestructible. The New Testament sheds more light concerning the spirit that continues to exist after death. Jesus committed His spirit to God at the end of His physical life (Luke 23:46), and Stephen did likewise (Acts 7:59).

The message also is that the spirit of a person will have to give an account of life's responsibilities before God after this life. The Teacher touches on this factor at the end, but here he anticipates the discussion.

Therefore, the young person must take to heart the fact that life is to be enjoyed, but physical life does not last forever; the body grows old, becomes infirm, and eventually gives out. It is one of the tragedies of the curse placed on man after his fall. No wonder the Teacher exclaims, "Meaningless! Meaningless! . . . Everything is meaningless!" (v. 8). He is not pessimistic in his world view. He has an even balance on the grasp of life that leads him to say that man should enjoy what he can, be circumspect and pious, and fear the Lord; but there is also the note of helplessness because the inexorable round of life finally does come to an end. Without controversy, everything about this world has the mark of impermanency. On this note the wise man ends his advice on how to best cope with this life and its problems, but he also anticipates what he will yet say in his epilogue.

For Further Study

1. Would the Teacher revise his observations about going to the house of mourning and that a sad face is good for the heart if he were writing from a New Testament perspective?

2. How do you relate what the Teacher said about how extortion and bribery can turn the heart of the wise man and the recent Abscam cases in which so many congressmen were involved?

3. Look up in a concordance a number of passages on patience that teach us the value of acquiring this desirable trait.

4. How do you suppose German Christians in heavily populated urban areas would have felt while living in the midst of the heavy bombing during World War II? How would they have rationalized it?

5. Research the various commentaries indicated in the Bibliography to find their interpretations of what it means to not be overrighteous, overwise, and overwicked.

6. Using a concordance and a Bible dictionary, try to find a number of passages in the Old Testament that suggest that man has a sin nature. The point is not to collect many passages that illustrate this belief but to find specific verses such as 7:20 that treat this aspect of man's being.

7. Read the Dialogue of Euthyphro by Plato. Would you say that the

search for ultimate definitions is somewhat the same as what the Teacher was asserting?

8. Research the commentaries concerning 7:28. Is there a relationship between what the Teacher said in 7:28–29 and 1 Timothy 2:11–15?

9. Discuss whether Christians do have the right to resist, either passively or violently, an evil and immoral government.

10. On the matter of obedience to the king or a nation's rulership, discuss whether the American colonists had a "right" to revolt against the British king over the tax issue.

11. List some examples from biblical sources of how the wicked were honored by the king or civil authorities and how these evil people were even praised by religious leaders.

12. List Bible characters who suffered while not knowing exactly why.

13. As an antidote to the seeming pessimism in 9:5–6, list each of the facets of life in the following verses that we can enjoy.

14. Using a concordance, research the use of "chance" or the Hebrew *pega'* in the Old Testament. Can we say that from man's point of view there might be an element of mystery, but from God's point of view the events form a part of His plan? Why or why not?

15. Since only select verses have been provided for the characteristics of the fool (*kesil*), research with a concordance and Bible dictionary the basic meaning and usages of *kesil*.

16. What should be the role of Christians living under oppressive, Marxist regimes that often also are corrupt, such as Poland?

17. From what the Teacher had to say concerning wisdom, kings, and rulers in 10:16–19, would you agree that there is a parallel in modern times with our own country? If so, in what ways?

18. How can the work ethic of 11:1–6 be applied today in families and schools so that young people will become industrious and responsible citizens?

19. Go through Ecclesiastes, and make a list of the many times the Teacher tells us to enjoy life.

20. To what idea or philosophy do we attribute the teaching that the joys of this world are worldly? The Manichean influence in the early church and Plato's philosophy with its emphasis on the real existence of the Forms in the next world can be clues to this research.

21. Why would the Teacher's description of the onset of old age with all its infirmities make an unforgettable sermonic picture?

Chapter 5

Epilogue
(Ecclesiastes 12:9–14)

Various commentators question the authenticity of the Epilogue from the hand of the Teacher. From the Introduction we have seen how several suggested that some scribe added his comments to the end of the book to provide an apology for its acceptance. It is wrong to overlook the connection of the book up to this point with the Epilogue and to suggest that the information in the Epilogue gives us a picture of the knowledge and character of the person who could write about the many experiences of life. He certainly did not need anyone to explain him; the Teacher can fend well for himself! As Delitzsch stated, "the spirit and tone of the book and of the epilogue are one" (p. 430).

A. The Teacher's Qualifications (12:9–10)

The Teacher calls himself wise (v. 9). Is he bragging? Although he did not use the first person but rather described himself in the third person which indicates an aspect of modesty, he did not have to apologize for the wisdom God gave him.

We have already identified Solomon as the Teacher; God gave him wisdom when he asked for it as a young man about to embark in his kingship over Israel. Solomon gave us 3,000 proverbs (1 Kings 4:32), and Proverbs 1–24 attest to his activity as a collector and composer of them. Why should we doubt this interest when he presided over the arts that included literature? Proverbs 25–29 are also Solomon's, collected at a later date by another patron of the arts, Hezekiah (Prov. 25:1). Therefore, what he wrote were right words, that is, delightful words, upright and true for correction in righteousness (v. 10). When we ponder the subject matter of Proverbs, we recognize a reflection of a wisdom that commended a moral for every phase of life. Certainly, the Teacher was well qualified. In addition, as we indicated in the Introduction, Ecclesiastes could have come only from the hand of a man well-advanced in years, a man who had tasted of the many experiences of life and was anxious to share the fruits of them.

B. Wisdom and Its Balance (12:11–12)

Two areas for consideration of the use of the words are now presented. They are like goads and firmly imbedded nails (v. 11). Goads were used to train cattle, to guide them in what the farmer wanted them to do (1 Sam. 13:21). The point is that the words of the wise, using good proverbs, are designed to prod the apathetic, the sluggish, and the naive or immature into action. The words set forth a moral and spiritual guidance for living godly in this world. All a person has to do to recognize this guidance is to see the purpose and theme of the Book of Proverbs (1:2–6) as well as the theme and many purposes of Ecclesiastes.

The phrase "collected sayings" has been interpreted as "masters of assemblies" or "councils of scholars." Gordis (p. 353) cites a number of traditional Jewish sources whereby the words of the wise are like goads and as nails driven in by the "masters of assemblies," or the words of the wise are like the fastened nails of the "councils of scholars," an interpretation which poses a difficulty (Delitzsch, pp. 432–35). It is best to leave the phrase as the NIV translated it. (See also Leupold, pp. 296–97.)

The collected sayings of the wise are likened to firmly imbedded nails, perhaps a reference to how the shepherds firmly anchored their tents. The point (a pointed pun!) is intended to emphasize that wisdom must be anchored firmly in a person's mental and spiritual makeup. One way or another, either by being prodded or firmly tied, we have to learn well the wisdom lessons in order to face life's problems with their stresses and strains. Israel had schools of wise men, as seen by Solomon and Hezekiah, in which a godly wisdom was set forth for the people.

The Teacher indicates that the words of wisdom, the collected sayings, all go back to one Source, the one Shepherd. The Lord is the Shepherd of Israel (Ps. 80:1); and in leading and guiding His people as His sheep, He is responsible for providing them with their physical and spiritual food, particularly wisdom based on His Word. It is interesting to note that the Teacher recognizes that God has been pleased to use him to impart a godly wisdom, and he declares that the words of wisdom are not the mouthings and prattlings of mere man. There is an authority behind wisdom. The warning, then, becomes quite clear: Take heed or be careful of what is more than or goes beyond what is taught in the words of the wise and their collected sayings. Israel had a special kind of wisdom from God and not a philosophy based on man's speculations and rationalizations. The Israelite had all that was necessary to help him face his world. Anything more or other than godly wisdom could have turned him away from faith in the Lord.

The term of endearment in verse 12, "My son," is very evident throughout the Book of Proverbs. It was the address to the young and inexperienced and carried with it the appeal to listen to the words of wisdom by the teachers of wisdom. In the same way, our Teacher admonishes us to listen intently to what he has to say and warns particularly that we should not turn away.

The reference to books without end and the fact that much study can weary the body is no doubt a description of the tremendous literary activity in the days of the Teacher. As indicated, this was a golden age in literature; and much energy was involved in all these efforts of writing and collecting many scrolls. By no means is there the suggestion that much study is ill-advised and that the making of many books is merely a waste of effort. He is stating a true fact that studying is wearying, but he does commend everyone to this task of studying the wisdom of God.

Israel subsequently was engaged in the production of a mass of literature besides the Old Testament; the years between the Testaments point to a tremendous activity in writing and the presence of numbers of books that people read avidly (Apocrypha, Pseudepigrapha, Qumran [Dead Sea] Scrolls and others). Paul reflected something of this interest when he called for the scrolls besides the parchments when he was in prison (2 Tim. 4:13). As long as the search for knowledge does not become the sole interest in life, we are encouraged to learn because it will help us put life in its proper perspective. The Book of Ecclesiastes is one instance of this interest.

C. The Key to Life: God Must Be in the Center (12:13–14)

The Teacher has now come to the end of his discourse, and we have to assert that he has covered a lot of ground. He began with the exclamation that all is vanity or meaningless, and we have seen that if we pursue any one area of interest that is exactly where we end—it is all meaninglessness. He has taken us through many thoughts and experiences regarding the gamut of life, at times seemingly pessimistic and at other times full of joy and anticipation. He has called us to be balanced people. If we seek for the essence or foundational understanding of wisdom, we will be frustrated; but we can have some knowledge and certain facets of understanding in this world. He has told us how to relate to people, to kings and governments, as well as with ourselves. He has warned us that we do grow old, our bodies become infirm, and eventually we will die, the body returning to the dust while the spirit returns to God. Therefore, he can say that he has come to the conclusion (v. 13). We wait with keen anticipation for his final words.

We are not kept in suspense long. The Teacher gives us a very important key to life and how we can be in the position to receive the wisdom of God. It is simply this: Fear God. The theme has been mentioned before (5:7; 7:18), but now he leaves us with the final word to remind us that God must be kept in the center of our lives. In all that we do, we must always be in reverential awe of God. All people and things are subservient to Him.

Not only are we to fear Him; we are encouraged to keep His commandments. In general, words like commandments, statutes, ordinances are all synonyms for God's Word. If we say that we know God or that His name is on our lips and at the same time we have no respect for His revealed will, then our words are mere superficiality. Not to follow through on what God asks us to do is a sham of life. As we stand in awe of Him and live His Word, we then understand that this is the whole duty of man. Literally, the last line of verse 13 reads, "For this is the whole of man," a wholeness with which man needs to be concerned and engaged. Here is where we will find reality as well as truly know ourselves. If the wholeness of man is in the interests and things of this world, then his very being becomes twisted and perverted. Only a solid tie with God can lead a person to total fulfillment.

Another reason concerning this exhortation to stand in awe before God is that we will have to give an account of ourselves (v. 14). Nothing hidden will remain hidden; everything will be revealed some day, the good as well as the evil. If there is one area that clearly defines the Teacher as far above any pessimism or Epicureanism, it is this call to a moral responsibility. While he calls us to enjoy life as we can, the chief end of man is not mere pleasure as many Greek philosophies proposed. The chief end of man is to honor God and serve Him. We must not say that he concludes on an ominous note. Rather, it is a high note because the Person of God is real, and man needs to reflect His righteousness in this world.

Our response is to give praise to God that we have a particular book of the Bible that gives us the best possible wisdom as to how to live in this world, keeping God in the center of everything we do. Bless His name forever and forever for this portion of revelation!

For Further Study

1. Using the commentaries listed in the Bibliography, research the meaning of the "words of the wise" and "their collected sayings."

2. Review from the entire Book of Ecclesiastes the distinctiveness of the wisdom that comes from God and how it differs from philosophical rationalization.

3. List from the wisdom literature—Job, Proverbs, Ecclesiastes, Psalms with a wisdom emphasis—the passages that declare that we are to fear God. In addition, indicate some of the implications that are mentioned; for example, in Proverbs 1:7 fools, because they do not fear the Lord, despise wisdom and discipline.

Bibliography

Archer, Gleason. "The Linguistic Evidence for the Date of 'Ecclesiastes,'" *Journal of the Evangelical Theological Society,* 12 (Summer 1969), pp. 167–181. See also *A Survey of Old Testament Introduction* (Chicago: Moody Press, 1964).

Barton, George A. *A Critical and Exegetical Commentary on the Book of Ecclesiastes* in *The International Critical Commentary,* eds. S. R. Driver, A. Plummer, C. A. Briggs (Edinburgh: T. & T. Clark, 1959).

Cohen, A. and Reichert, V., eds. "Ecclesiastes," *The Five Megillot* (London: The Soncino Press, 1952).

Delitzsch, F. "Song of Songs and Ecclesiastes," *Commentaries on the Old Testament* (Grand Rapids: Eerdmans, 1950).

Hengstenberg, E. W. *Commentary on Ecclesiastes,* tr. D. W. Simon (Philadelphia: Smith, English, 1860).

Genung, John F. *Words of Koheleth* (New York: Houghton, Mifflin, 1904).

Ginsberg, David Christian. *The Song of Solomon and Coheleth* (New York: KTAV, 1970).

Gordis, Robert. *Koheleth, The Man and His World* (New York: Schocken, 1968).

Kaiser, Walter. *Ecclesiastes: Total Life* (Chicago: Moody Press, 1979).

Leupold, H. C. *Exposition of Ecclesiastes* (Grand Rapids: Baker, 1952).

Whybray, R. N. "Qoheleth the Immoralist? (Qoh. 7:16–17)," *Israelite Wisdom: Theological and Literary Essays in Honor of Samuel Terrein,* ed. John Gammie (Missoula, MT: Scholars, 1978).

Wright, J. Stafford. "The Interpretation of Ecclesiastes," *Evangelical Quarterly,* 18 (January 15, 1946), pp. 18–34.